2ND EDITION
WORKBOOK

T0351695

Contents

Kids in My Class

Vocabulary

1 **Read and look. Write the names.**

Julia is serious. She likes to read. She has blond hair.

Tony has short black hair. He's very friendly and funny.

Amelia has straight hair. She's shy and plays the flute.

José is friendly and smart. He has brown hair and wears glasses.

1 _____ 2 _____ 3 _____ 4 _____

2 **Look at 1 and circle T for true or F for false.**

1	José wears glasses.	T	F
2	Amelia has wavy hair.	T	F
3	Julia has brown hair.	T	F
4	Tony is friendly.	T	F
5	Amelia is shy.	T	F
6	Tony is serious.	T	F
7	José has black hair.	T	F
8	Julia likes to read.	T	F

11
3 Listen and write.

Who's That Girl?

It's the first day of school.
We're back in our classes.
Everybody looks different,
And I have new ¹_____!

Who's that girl
Standing over there?
She's taller ²_____ me.
She has ³_____ dark hair.

In my class are the same friends I know.
But we all change. We all grow. (x2)

It's the first day of school,
And I'm back in my chair.
Everybody looks different.
Now I have ⁴_____ hair.

Who's that girl?
Oh, wait, that's Marie!
Last time I saw her,
She was ⁵_____ than me!

Chorus

4 What are you like? Write.

_____
_____
_____
_____
_____

How did I do? ☆☆☆☆☆

Story

5   Read. Then choose the correct answer.

She's Just Like You!

There's a new girl in our class.

Oh, really? What's she like?

Her name's Amanda. She has curly dark hair.

Just like yours!

Is she nice?

Yes, she's nice. And she's smart, too. But she's also a little shy.

1   ___ is a new student.
    a Amanda   **b** Cristina

2   ___ and her dad are talking about the new student.
    a Amanda   **b** Cristina

3   ___ curly dark hair.
    a Amanda has   **b** Cristina has
    c Amanda and Cristina have

4   ___ is nice, smart, and shy.
    a Amanda   **b** Cristina

6   Think about a classmate. Answer the questions.

1   What's his/her name?   _____

2   What color is his/her hair?   _____

3   Is he/she tall or short?   _____

4   Is his/her hair long or short?   _____

Think of a person in your family. What do they look like? What are they like?

_____

How did I do? ☆☆☆☆☆

7 Listen and ✓.

1 Ruby is

⬜ **a** taller than Martin's dad.

⬜ **b** shorter than Martin's dad.

2 Philip has

⬜ **a** short hair.

⬜ **b** long hair.

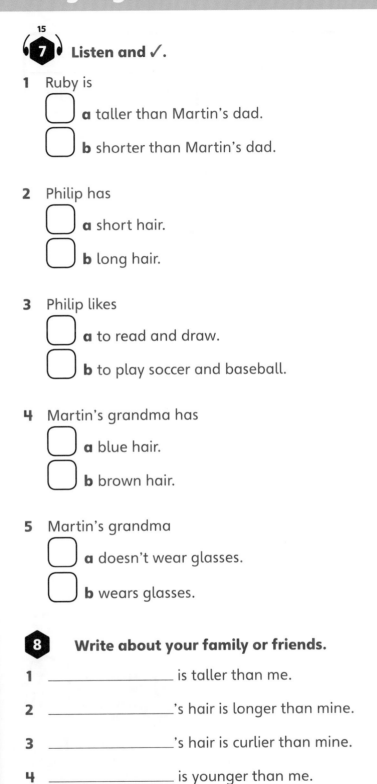

3 Philip likes

⬜ **a** to read and draw.

⬜ **b** to play soccer and baseball.

4 Martin's grandma has

⬜ **a** blue hair.

⬜ **b** brown hair.

5 Martin's grandma

⬜ **a** doesn't wear glasses.

⬜ **b** wears glasses.

8 Write about your family or friends.

1 _____ is taller than me.

2 _____'s hair is longer than mine.

3 _____'s hair is curlier than mine.

4 _____ is younger than me.

How did I do? ☆☆☆☆☆

Grammar

old	→	old**er**
big	→	big**ger**
heavy	→	heav**ier**

> Who is **bigger**, Chris or Tom?   Chris is **bigger than** Tom.

9   **Complete the sentences.**

1 Maddie is _____taller_____ than Henry. (tall)

2 Valerie is _____ than I am. (old)

3 My mom's hair is _____ than mine. (curly)

4 My school is _____ than my brother's. (big)

5 This book is _____ than that one. (small)

6 Jon's eyes are _____ than mine. (light)

10   **Look at 9. Copy the sentences. Then complete the new sentences.**

1 Maddie is taller than Henry.

Henry is _____shorter_____ than Maddie.

2 Valerie is older than I am.

I am _____younger_____ than Valerie.

3 _____

My hair is _____ than my mom's.

4 _____

My brother's school is _____ than mine.

5 _____

That book is _____ than this one.

6 _____

My eyes are _____ than Jon's.

How did I do? ☆ ☆ ☆ ☆ ☆

My sister's hair is longer than **my hair**.	My sister's hair is longer than **mine**.
My sister's hair is longer than **your hair**.	My sister's hair is longer than **yours**.

11 **Match the meanings.**

1 Bob's friends are older than **our friends**.   mine

2 Our backpacks are heavier than **their backpacks**.   yours

3 Your father is smarter than **my father**.   hers

4 Jose's hair is straighter than **his sister's hair**.   ours

5 My eyes are darker than **your eyes**.   theirs

12 **Complete the sentences.**

> hers   mine   ours   theirs   yours
> shorter   smaller   smarter   taller   younger

1 **Our dog** is smart, but your dog is very smart.

Your dog is ___smarter___ than ___ours___.

2 Your class has 12 students. It's small. **Their class** has 15 students.

Your class is _____ than _____.

3 His cousin is four feet tall. **My cousin** is only three feet tall.

His cousin is _____ than _____.

4 Juan's hair is short. **Kate's hair** is long.

Juan's hair is _____ than _____.

5 **Your sister** is 10. His sister is 7.

His sister is _____ than _____.

How did I do? ☆☆☆☆☆

13 **Complete the sentences.**

| chance | common | fraternal | identical | triplets |

1 A mother gives birth to Maria and Martin together. They don't look alike.

They are _____ twins.

2 A mother gives birth to Tina, Gina, and Nina together. They are _____.

3 A mother gives birth to Bob and Rob together. They look the same. They are

_____ twins.

4 Fraternal twins are more _____ than identical twins.

5 The _____ of having triplets is 1 in every 625 births.

17
 14 **Listen, read, and circle. Which animal can have the most babies at one time?**

Some scientists say the chance of having [1]**fraternal / identical** quadruplets is only 1 in 13 million. Not if you're a nine-banded armadillo! These armadillo moms give birth to up to 56 pups in their lifetime. And every time they give birth, they have FOUR identical babies at a time. That means that an average armadillo has a record-breaking fourteen sets of [2]**triplets / quadruplets**. That's impossible for humans and very [3]**rare / common** in the animal kingdom.

[4]**Multiple / Single** births are very common in the animal kingdom. Often, this is because not all the babies survive. Cats usually give birth to 3–5 kittens, and some dogs have 5–10 puppies. These little brothers and sisters look alike, just like brothers and sisters in human multiple births, but they are very rarely identical.

Other animals rarely or never have multiple births. Usually, [5]**smaller / bigger** animals have more babies and larger animals have fewer. Elephants have only one baby at a time. Whales almost always have only one baby at a time. These animals have a very different relationship with their offspring.

However, pigs are different. They are larger than other farm animals, but they have a lot of babies. Sometimes they have 20 piglets at a time!

nine-banded armadillo

How did I do? ☆☆☆☆☆

15 **Look at 14 and choose the correct answer.**

1 Nine-banded armadillos always have

   a identical quadruplets.   **b** fraternal quadruplets.

2 How many times does a nine-banded armadillo give birth in a lifetime?

   a up to 14   **b** up to 56

3 Which animal never has triplets?

   a an elephant   **b** a cat

4 Which animals usually have more babies?

   a small animals   **b** big animals

5 Which animal almost always has only one baby at a time?

   a a dog   **b** a whale

6 Pigs are unusual because

   a they don't have multiple births.   **b** they're large and they have many babies at once.

16 **Complete the sentences.**

| alike | birth | fingerprints | rare | relationship | survive |

1 You and your brother don't look _____. He's much darker than you.

2 Red hair is very _____ now – not many people have it.

3 Identical twins are not completely identical. They have different _____.

4 Pigs sometimes give _____ to 20 piglets.

5 Small animals have multiple births because they want some of them to _____.

6 The _____ between twins begins before they're born.

How did I do? ☆☆☆☆☆

17 Read the text in the Student's Book and complete the sentences.

chonmage	beards	powdered wigs	braids	dyed wigs

1 Women in ancient Egypt wore _____.

2 Men in ancient Egypt sometimes wore fake _____.

3 Judges in the U.K. wear _____.

4 Some men and women in Africa have _____.

5 Sumo wrestlers in Japan have a special hairstyle called _____.

18 Look at 17. Number the pictures.

a  b  c  d  e

19 Look at 18 and write T for true and F for false.

1 The African woman's hair is longer than the judge's wig.

2 The ancient Egyptian woman's wig is brighter than the judge's wig.

3 The sumo wrestler's hair is darker than the ancient Egyptian woman's wig.

4 The judge's wig is straighter than the sumo wrestler's hair.

20 Look at 18 and 19. Compare your hair with one of the pictures. Write sentences with than mine.

short	long	light	dark	straight	curly	wavy

1 The African woman's hair is shorter than mine. _____

2 _____

3 _____

How did I do? ☆ ☆ ☆ ☆ ☆

21 **Read and number the parts of the paragraph.**

My Best Friend ← 1

My best friend's name is James. ← 2

He's shorter than I am, and his hair is darker than mine. James is shy, and he's ← 3
funny, too. We like playing soccer on the weekend.

I'm happy to have a friend like James. ← 4

a detail sentences ☐   **b** final sentence ☐

c title ☐   **d** topic sentence ☐

22 **Read the paragraph. Circle the detail sentences. Copy the topic and final sentences.**

Mr. Smith is my favorite teacher. He's the music teacher at my school. He can sing! He also plays the piano and the guitar. He's also very smart, and he's funny, too. I'm happy to have a teacher like Mr. Smith.

Topic sentence: _____

_____

Final sentence: _____

_____

23 **Look at 22. Write about a favorite teacher.**

Topic sentence: _____

Detail 1: _____

Detail 2: _____

Detail 3: _____

Final sentence: _____

24 **Read and circle ear and air.**

year   fair   skirt

curly   pair   hear

chair   taller   more

hair   fear

25 **Underline the words with ear and air. Then read aloud.**

1 She has small ears and curly fair hair.

2 I hear a pair of twins near the stairs.

26 **Connect the letters. Then write.**

1 y   air   **a** __ __ __ __ __

2 ch   ear   **b** __ __ __ __

23

 27 **Listen and write.**

A boy with big ¹_____
And ²_____ hair
Hears the twins on the
³_____
A boy with big ears and fair
⁴_____
⁵_____ the twins sit on
their chairs.

How did I do? ☆☆☆☆☆

Review

28 **Read and match.**

1 Twins are the

2 Identical twins look

3 Triplets are more

a common than quadruplets.

b most common.

c the same.

29 **Look and complete the sentences.**

glasses	serious
shorter	straight
taller	wavy

1 Mom's hair is _____.

2 Dad's hair is _____.

3 Mia is _____ than Tim.

4 Tim is _____ than Mia.

5 Grandma wears _____.

6 Mia likes to read. She is _____.

30 **Complete the sentences.**

 My hair is longer than yours.

His hair is shorter than mine.

1 My hair is longer than yours.
Your hair is shorter

_____.

2 Your brother is taller than mine.
My brother is shorter

_____.

3 His hair is curlier than hers.
Her hair is straighter

_____.

4 Her legs are shorter than his.
His legs are longer

_____.

5 Our car is cheaper than theirs.
Their car is more expensive

_____.

6 Their house is smaller than ours.
Our house is bigger

_____.

How did I do? ☆ ☆ ☆ ☆ ☆

2 Our Schedule

Vocabulary

1 Look and write.

> eat out   go on vacation   go to the dentist
> help clean   shop for food   watch a movie

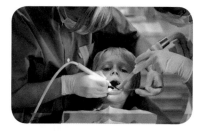

1 _____

2 _____

3 _____

4 _____

5 _____

6 _____

2 Read and circle the correct answer.

1 I brush my teeth twice a **morning** / **day**.

2 I walk the dog every **week** / **afternoon**.

3 We walk to school every **morning** / **year**.

4 We visit our grandparents every **hour** / **month**.

5 We go skiing every **summer** / **winter**.

6 I take dance lessons once a **morning** / **week**.

Song

Things We Do!

There are a lot of things
That I do every day,
Like go to school, ¹**have / watch** a movie,
Stay up late, and play!

But there are a lot of other things
I don't want to do so much,
Like ²**go / see** to the dentist, ³**make / do** the dishes,
⁴**Make / Do** my bed, and such.

How often do you do these things?
Every day? Once a week? Once a year?

I ⁵**take in / take out** the trash
On Tuesdays before school.
And I feed our funny cat,
But I don't mind – she's cool.

Chorus

4 **What about you? Complete the chart.**

once a day	I _____
twice a day	I _____
every night	I _____
every summer	I _____

How did I do? ☆☆☆☆☆

5 **Read. Then circle.**

A Lot of Weddings!

What are you doing this weekend, Amanda?

I'm going to my grandma's house.

How often do you see your grandma?

Every Saturday.

How about you? What are you doing this weekend?

I'm going to my cousin's wedding.

1 Amanda is going to her **cousin's / grandma's** house.

2 Amanda sees her grandma once a **week / month**.

3 Christina is going to her **brother's / cousin's** wedding.

6 **Now answer the questions about you.**

1 How often do you visit your grandma? _____

2 How often do you go to weddings? _____

3 What are you doing this weekend? _____

every day   every Friday   once a year
three times a month   twice a day

THINK BIG

Think and write in order.

not very often ➤ _____ ➤ _____ ➤ _____ ➤ _____ ➤ _____ very often

_____ _____ _____ _____ _____

How did I do? ☆ ☆ ☆ ☆ ☆

Language in Action

7 Listen and complete the sentences.

1   Mindy and her dad are going to the supermarket Saturday _____.

2   Julian and Billy are going to the movies _____ afternoon.

3   Jenna sees her cousins four _____ a year.

4   Suzanne has soccer practice three times a _____.

5   Joey walks his dog _____ a day.

8   Read and match.

1
What are you doing this weekend?

a
About once a week.

2
How often do you eat pizza?

b
They're going to the zoo.

3
Where are they going this afternoon?

c
I'm going to the movies.

How did I do? ☆ ☆ ☆ ☆ ☆

Grammar

Where is	he/she	going after school?	He/She	is going to soccer practice.
What are	you	doing tonight?	I	am watching a movie at home.
			We	are watching a movie at home.
	they		They	

9   **Circle the correct word.**

1   **What / Where** are they doing after school?

2   **What / Where** is she doing tomorrow?

3   **What / Where** are your friends going this summer?

4   **What / Where** is he doing after school?

5   **What / Where** are you doing Saturday morning?

6   **What / Where** are we going on vacation?

10   **Look at the questions in 9. Write the answers.**

1   They're _____going_____ on vacation.

2   She's _____ her cousins.

3   They're _____ to Australia.

4   He's _____ soccer in the park.

5   I'm _____ my room.

6   We're _____ to China.

cleaning
going
going
going
playing
visiting

11   **Answer about you.**

1   What are you doing this weekend? _____

2   Where are you going after school? _____

How did I do? ☆ ☆ ☆ ☆ ☆

How often does	he/she	have guitar lessons?	Once a week. Twice a day. Every Friday. On Sundays. Once a month. Every summer.
How often do	you	go to the dentist?	
	they		

12 **Look at Laura's schedule. Answer the questions.**

This is my schedule.

every day   twice a day
once a week twice a week

	Sun	Mon	Tue	Wed	Thu	Fri	Sat
play outside	✗	✗	✗	✗	✗	✗	✗
brush teeth	✗✗	✗✗	✗✗	✗✗	✗✗	✗✗	✗✗
help with laundry					✗		
have piano lessons		✗		✗			

1 How often does Laura play outside? _____

2 How often does Laura brush her teeth? _____

3 How often does Laura help her parents with the laundry?

_____

4 How often does Laura have piano lessons? _____

13 **Write questions beginning with How often.**

1 _How often do_ _____ you go shopping?

2 _____ they play soccer?

3 _____ he eat pizza?

4 _____ you watch TV?

How did I do? ☆ ☆ ☆ ☆ ☆

14   **Read and match.**

1   Lucy has a lot of friends.

2   This is something I buy.

3   These are big posters by the side of the road.

4   This makes you want to buy something.

a   It's a product.

b   They're billboards.

c   It's an advertisement.

d   She's popular.

15   36   **Listen, read, and circle. What do children love?**

Advertising

Buy it now! Only $2.99

Washes whiter and faster

Cristiano Ronaldo's favorite cereal

For a healthy and happy life

When big companies are going to make an ad, they use four things to make us buy.

For cereals and different foods, they create a cartoon ¹**character / person**. Children love cartoon characters. When children see them, they want to buy!

For products like sneakers, coffee, and perfume, they choose ²**famous / well-known** actors and athletes. We like to buy the things that these people use.

Companies use other ³**tools / tunes** for selling, too. Things we can read or hear. For example, they use ⁴**slogans / advertisements**. They're catchy phrases we can't forget when we think about a product.

Companies also use images with ⁵**bright / attractive** colors and great photos. Exciting billboards help sell products because they catch our ⁶**eye / nose** and make us think about the product.

16   **Look at 15. Read and write.**

| buy   cereal   images   forget |

1   Cartoons help sell _____ to children.

2   We like to _____ the products athletes use.

3   When a slogan is good, we can't _____ the words.

4   Eye-catching _____ on billboards help sell products.

How did I do?

17 Look at the advertisement. Read and circle **T** for true and **F** for false.

advertisement

I love **123 Juice** because it tastes delicious. Miss Lulu drinks it. She's my favorite singer. All my friends like it. We drink it together at parties and in school. We always sing the song: **1, 2, 3, Drink with me. 1, 2, 3, Drink with me.** It's a catchy tune!

1 This ad uses a cartoon character to sell the product. **T** **F**

2 It uses a jingle to help you remember the product. **T** **F**

3 It tells you it will make you popular. **T** **F**

18 Complete the sentences. Use the words from the box.

> catch   company   slogan   tune

1 I like that _____. I can't stop singing it!

2 Your dress is amazing. It's going to _____ everyone's eye!

3 My dad works for a big soda _____ in New York.

4 The _____ for their soda is "The Taste You Have in Mind." That's really catchy.

How did I do? ☆ ☆ ☆ ☆ ☆

19 **Read the text in the Student's Book and complete the sentences. Write your answer.**

actions	beliefs	connection	luck

Superstitions are ¹_____ that there's a
²_____ between two ³_____.
For example, some people in the U.K. believe that
it's bad ⁴_____ to walk under a ladder.
When I have a test, I use my lucky pen. Do you have
a lucky item? What is it?

_____
_____
_____

20 **Look at page 23 of the Student's Book. Write GL for good luck and BL for bad luck.**

Superstitions in some countries bring good or bad luck. Which do these bring?

1 I eat 12 grapes on New Year's Eve. _____

2 He cuts his fingernails in the dark. _____

3 She carries an empty bucket. _____

4 They live on the fourth floor. _____

5 We sleep in a closed room with a fan on. _____

21 **Draw and write about a superstition in your country.**

You should / shouldn't

_____.

It brings _____ luck.

How did I do? ☆ ☆ ☆ ☆ ☆

22   **Read and circle the sequence words.**

> **My Day at School**
>
> First, we have math. Next, we have a spelling test. Then we have lunch. After that, we have English class. Finally, we have P.E.

23   **Read the paragraph. Look at 22. Write the sequence words.**

I am busy after school. ¹_____,
I have a snack. ²_____, I walk my
dog. ³_____ I play outside.
⁴_____, I eat dinner.
⁵_____, I do the dishes with my
brother and my dad.

24   **What do you do after school? Add two more activities. Then number the six activities in order and write a paragraph.**

☐ do homework   ☐ have a snack   ☐ _____

☐ eat dinner   ☐ play games   ☐ _____

How did I do? ☆ ☆ ☆ ☆ ☆

25   **Read and circle ir and ur.**

> **bird**   shirt   **fur**
>
> **dear**   stairs   curl
>
> ear   **hurt**   **skirt**
>
> girl   surf

26   **Underline the words with ir and ur. Then read aloud.**

1   The girl is wearing a short skirt and a long T-shirt.

2   Pandas have black and white fur.

27   **Connect the letters. Then write.**

1   s   urn   **a** _ _ _ _

2   t   urf   **b** _ _ _ _

3   b   urt   **c** _ _ _ _

4   h   ird   **d** _ _ _ _

28 ⁴² **Listen and write.**

> Two **1**_____ with red
> **2**_____ ,
> Two cats with black **3**_____ ,
> Two boys with white **4**_____
> Are watching **5**_____ !

How did I do? ☆☆☆☆☆

29 **Complete the dialog.**

| After that | doing | First | going | What | Where |

Ana: Hey, José! ¹_____ are you doing after school?

José: I'm really busy. ²_____, I'm visiting my grandma.

Ana: Then what are you ³_____?

José: Then I'm meeting my mom.

Ana: ⁴_____ are you going?

José: We're ⁵_____ to the dentist.

Ana: Oh, no.

José: That's okay. ⁶_____, we're going to the movies!

30 **Complete the questions. Then write answers. Use words from the box.**

| do the dishes/twice a week | go on vacation/twice a year |
| play outside/every day | watch a movie/once a week |

1

How often _does he do the dishes_____?

He _____.

2

How often _____?

_____

3

How often _____?

_____

4

How often do they _____?

_____

Food Around the World

Vocabulary

1 **Look and match. Write the letter.**

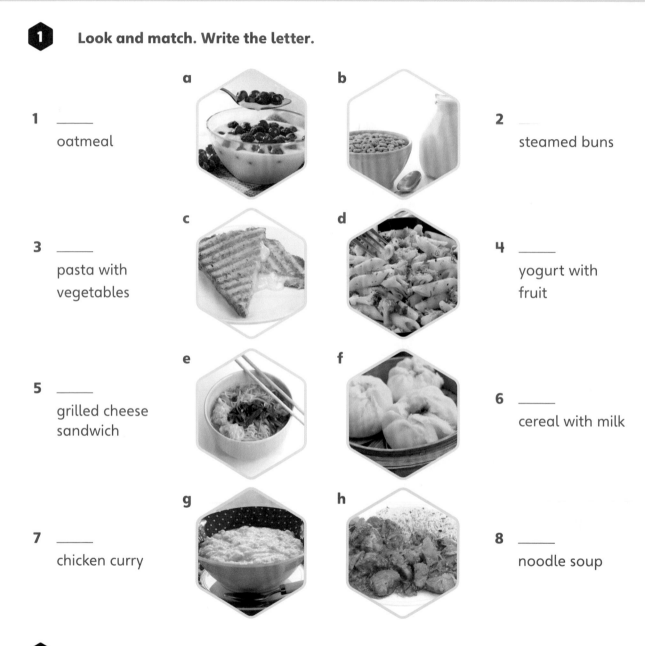

1 _____ oatmeal

2 _____ steamed buns

3 _____ pasta with vegetables

4 _____ yogurt with fruit

5 _____ grilled cheese sandwich

6 _____ cereal with milk

7 _____ chicken curry

8 _____ noodle soup

2 **What foods do you like?**

Breakfast: _____

Lunch: _____

Dinner: _____

49

3 Listen and number in order. Which food is in the song? Put a ✓ or a ✗.

Would You Like Some?

"Come on, Sam. Just one little bite!"
"Oh, really, Dad. Oh, all right!
Mmm. Hey, you're right. It's great!
Please put some more on my plate!"

Come on, Sam, please have a little taste!
Come on, Sam, don't make a funny face!

"Would you like some chicken curry?"
"No, thanks, Dad. I'm in a hurry!"
Sam says, "No, Dad, not right now.
But thanks so much – thanks, anyhow."

"How about a sweet steamed bun?
It's really yummy. Come on, try one!"
Sam says, "No, Dad, not right now.
But thanks so much – thanks, anyhow."

Chorus

"Would you like some noodle soup?
Tonight it tastes really nice!"
Sam says, "No, Dad, not right now.
But thanks so much – thanks, anyhow."

4 Correct the strange food and write.

1 steamed cereal _____

2 oatmeal curry _____

3 toasted yogurt sandwich _____

4 apple soup _____

5 milk with lemonade _____

How did I do? ☆☆☆☆☆

Story

5   Read. Then circle T for true or F for false.

Homemade Lemonade

1	Christina likes Sam's cake.	T	F
2	Christina thinks the lemonade tastes good.	T	F
3	The lemonade is sweet.	T	F
4	Sam put lemons in his lemonade.	T	F
5	Sam forgot to put sugar in his lemonade.	T	F

6   Write about you. Answer Yes, I would or No, I wouldn't.

1   Would you like to drink some lemon juice?   _____

2   Would you like to eat some chocolate cake?   _____

3   Would you like to drink some lemonade?   _____

THINK BIG

What happens next in the story? Write.

_____

_____

7 *53* **Listen and ✓ the answers.**

1 Pablo would like

◻ chicken fried rice.

◻ rice and beans.

◻ pizza.

2 The vegetable curry is

◻ salty.

◻ sour.

◻ spicy.

3 Grandma would like

◻ yogurt with fruit and sugar.

◻ yogurt with fruit.

◻ fruit with sugar.

4 Anna-Marie thinks the corn tortillas are

◻ salty.   ◻ spicy.   ◻ sweet.

5 The girl likes

◻ orange juice.   ◻ lemonade.   ◻ water.

8 **Answer about you.**

1 I like food that is

◻ salty.   ◻ sour.   ◻ spicy.   ◻ sweet.

2 What would you like for dinner?

I'd like _____.

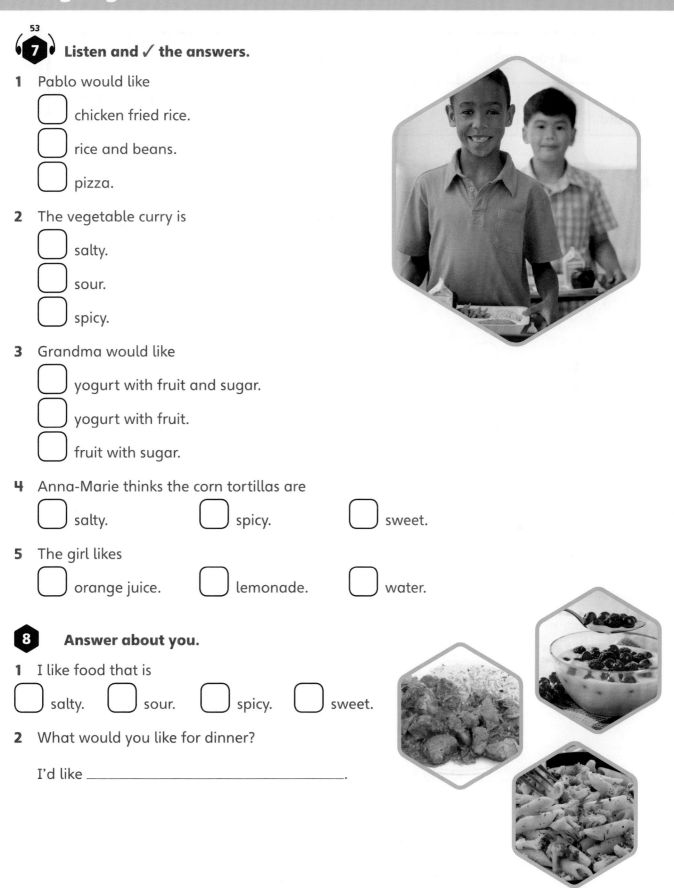

How did I do? ☆☆☆☆☆

Grammar

What **would** you **like**?			I'd **like** some soup.		I'd like → I would like
What **would**	he/she	**like**?	He**'d**/She**'d**	**like** yogurt.	He'd/She'd like → He/She would like

9 Listen and ✓. Then complete the sentences.

Name: _____	Name: _____	Name: _____
Drinks	**Drinks**	**Drinks**
lemonade ☐	lemonade ☐	lemonade ☐
apple juice ☐	apple juice ☐	apple juice ☐
milk ✓	milk ☐	milk ☐
Lunch	**Lunch**	**Lunch**
chicken curry ☐	chicken curry ☐	chicken curry ☐
noodle soup ✓	noodle soup ☐	noodle soup ☐
rice and beans ☐	rice and beans ☐	rice and beans ☐
steamed buns ☐	steamed buns ☐	steamed buns ☐

1 What _____would_____ Linda _____like_____?

   She'd like milk and noodle soup.

2 What _____ Paul _____?

   _____

3 What _____ Maria _____?

   _____

10 Look at 9. Write about you. What would you like?

   _____

How did I do? ☆ ☆ ☆ ☆ ☆

Would	you	**like to try** some curry?	Yes,	I	would.	No,	I	wouldn't.
	he/she			we			we	
				he/she			he/she	
	they			they			they	

11 **Look at the pictures. Complete the sentences.**

1

A: ___Would___ she ___like___ to have some pasta?

B: ___No___, she ___wouldn't___.

2

A: _____ he _____ to eat some oatmeal?

B: _____, he _____.

3

A: _____ they _____ to drink mango smoothies?

B: _____, they _____.

4

A: _____ they _____ to try some curry?

B: _____, they _____.

12 **Write about you.**

1 A: _____ you _____ to try _____?

B: Yes, I _____.

2 A: _____ you _____ to try _____?

B: No, I _____.

How did I do? ☆ ☆ ☆ ☆ ☆

13 **Circle the correct words.**

1 For **a balanced** / **an unhealthy** diet, eat food from each of the five food groups every day.

2 The five food groups are: fruit, vegetables, dairy, protein, and **chicken** / **grains**.

3 Eat more **vegetables** / **dairy** than protein.

4 Don't eat food that is too **tasty** / **salty**.

5 Don't have too many **sugary** / **fresh** drinks.

14 **Listen, read, and complete. Which food can be both low-fat and full-fat?**

| balance | bigger | five | grains | guide | smaller | sugar |

We need to eat a balanced diet. That means we should eat foods from each of the ¹_____ food groups every day. The main food groups are grains, vegetables, fruit, protein, and dairy.

Look at the My Plate picture. This shows the amount of each food group we should eat. It's very important to get the right ²_____.

The vegetables section is ³_____ than all the others. So we should eat more of them than any other food. The ⁴_____ section is also very important. We need to eat a little more of them than protein. Fruit is also important, but it has a lot of ⁵_____ in it, so we can't eat too much. And dairy foods aren't always low-fat. A lot of dairy foods can make us fat. That's why the dairy section is ⁶_____ than all the others.

Would you like to be healthier? Then remember to always use My Plate as a ⁷_____ at mealtimes.

My Plate

15 **Look at 14. Circle T for true or F for false.**

1 We don't need to eat all five food groups every day. T F

2 Put mostly protein on your plate. T F

3 It's bad to eat too much fruit. T F

4 It's better to eat low-fat dairy foods. T F

5 My Plate is a very useful guide. T F

How did I do? ☆ ☆ ☆ ☆ ☆

16 **Match the words and definitions.**

1 This is the word we use for all the foods we choose to eat.

2 We describe chips and fries with this word.

3 We describe candy, cupcakes, and soda with this word.

4 Chicken and fish are healthy sources of this.

5 Cheese contains a lot of this.

a fat

b protein

c salty

d diet

e sugary

17 **Write the food on the plate.**

bananas   beans   bread   carrots   cereal
cheese   chicken   fish   mangoes   milk
oranges   pasta   peppers   potatoes   rice   yogurt

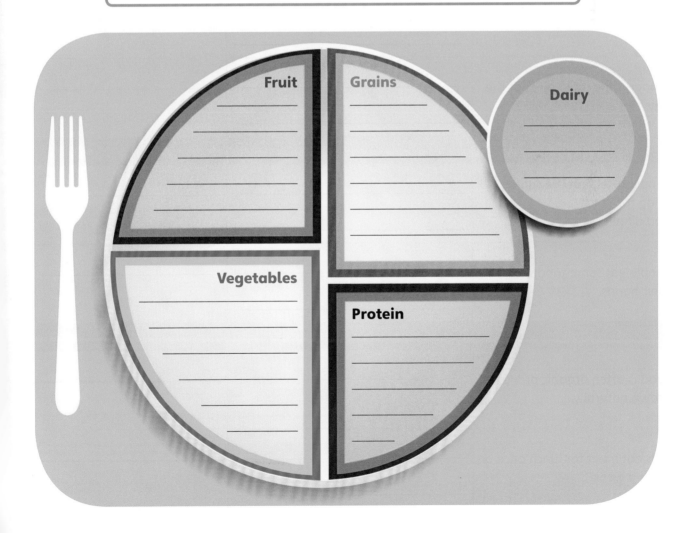

Fruit

Grains

Dairy

Vegetables

Protein

18 Read about school lunches on page 35 of your Student's Book. Then write about *your* school lunches. What's the same/different?

What do they eat for lunch in England?

Japan	_____ (my country)	Same or Different?
Kids take turns serving.		
Kids eat lunch in their classroom.		
England		
Most kids bring sandwiches from home.		
Dinner is the main meal of the day.		
Zambia		
People often eat the same thing for lunch and dinner.		
People eat some food with their hands.		
Italy		
Food is often organic or grown naturally.		
Kids eat meat for lunch once or twice a week.		

How did I do? ☆ ☆ ☆ ☆ ☆

19 **Read and write so or because.**

1 I love eating paella, _____ I have it twice a week.

2 I don't like eating chicken curry _____ I don't like spicy food.

20 **Read and match. Then circle the conjunctions.**

1 She doesn't like milk,

a so we eat them every week.

2 It's cold today,

b because I want to be healthy.

3 I often have a toasted cheese sandwich for breakfast

c so I'm having oatmeal for breakfast.

4 We love eating meatballs,

d because rice is his favorite food.

5 Carlos likes paella

e so she doesn't drink it.

6 I eat a balanced diet

f because I like cheese a lot.

21 **Join the sentences and write. Use so and because.**

1 I'm wearing a coat. It's cold.

_____

2 I don't like fruit. I don't eat watermelon.

_____

3 Sally is happy. She's eating her favorite lunch.

_____

How did I do? ☆☆☆☆☆

22   **Read and circle le, el, al, and il.**

apple   curl   April

pencil   medal   sandal

hear

camel   hair

bubble   travel

23   **Underline the words with le, el, al, and il. Then read aloud.**

1   There are apples in April.

2   I wear sandals when I travel in the summer.

24   **Connect the letters. Then write.**

1   app   el   **a**   __ __ __ __ __

2   Apr   le   **b**   __ __ __ __ __

3   cam   al   **c**   __ __ __ __ __

4   med   il   **d**   __ __ __ __ __

25  **Listen and write.**

Take your ¹ _____.
Draw a ² _____.
Draw a ³ _____.
Draw some ⁴ _____.

How did I do? ☆ ☆ ☆ ☆ ☆

26 **Write questions or answers.**

1 **A:** What would she like for breakfast?

B: _____

2 **A:** _____

B: He'd like a toasted cheese sandwich for lunch.

3 **A:** What would they like for dinner?

B: _____

4 **A:** _____

B: They'd like chicken curry for dinner.

?

5 **A:** What would you like for dinner?

B: _____

27 **Read and circle the correct words.**

Mom: **Would / Should** you like to go to an Indian restaurant?

Bobby: No, I **can't / wouldn't**.

Mom: **Let's / How about** an Italian restaurant?

Bobby: No, **let's / thanks**.

Mom: Well, where **can / would** you like to go?

Bobby: **I'd like / Let's go** to a candy store!

28 **Read and match.**

1 Eat more grains   **a** balanced diet.

2 Don't eat too   **b** much salt.

3 Have a lot of   **c** than protein.

4 Have a   **d** fruit.

How did I do? ☆ ☆ ☆ ☆ ☆

My Robot

1 Choose and draw one path. Design a robot.

2 Look at your path in 1. Answer the questions with words from your path.

What is the robot like?

What is it doing today?

What would it like to try?

3 Look at your path in 1 and ✓ the correct word or words.

My robot likes ☐ spicy ☐ salty ☐ sweet ☐ sour food.

MY NAME IS

_____.

END

4 Look at the information about your robot. Give it a name. Write a paragraph about it.

_____

_____

_____

_____

_____

_____

How Do You Feel?

Vocabulary

1 Complete the sentences.

> allergies   coughing   fever   headache
> sneezing   sore throat   stomachache

1 My mom has bad ⬜a ⬜l ⬜l ⬜e ⬜r ⬜g ⬜i ⬜e ⬜s .

2 Her eyes are watering and she's ◯⬜⬜⬜⬜⬜◯⬜ .

3 I have a cold. I'm ⬜⬜◯u⬜⬜◯⬜⬜ and I feel tired.

4 I have a really bad ⬜⬜⬜⬜⬜◯⬜⬜⬜⬜⬜ . I don't want to eat anything.

5 Your dad has a ⬜⬜⬜⬜⬜◯c⬜⬜ . Please turn off the TV.

6 Grandma has a bad ⬜⬜⬜◯ ⬜⬜⬜⬜⬜⬜ . She's drinking tea.

7 Your head feels hot. You must have a ⬜⬜⬜◯⬜ .

2 Write the letters from the circles in 1. Use the letters to complete the joke.

◯l ◯ ◯u ◯ ◯ ◯ ◯ ◯

Doctor, my son ate my pen! What should I do?

◯u ◯ ◯ ◯
◯p ◯ ◯ ◯ ◯l

Song

70

3 Listen and write. Use the words from the box.

Stay in Bed and Rest!

You're ¹_____
And you're ²_____.
You need to stay in bed.
I think you have a fever.
Here, let me feel your head.
You shouldn't go to school today.
You should ³_____ instead.

When you're sick or feeling blue,
Your family takes good care of you.

You have a ⁴_____
And a ⁵_____.
Here's what I suggest:
You should drink some ⁶_____
And juice.
⁷_____ and rest!
Listen to your dad, now,
Taking care of yourself is best.

Chorus

cold	coughing	fever
sneezing	stay home
stay in bed	tea

4 Read and choose the correct answer.

When you're sick, here's what I suggest:

1 You shouldn't
  a stay in bed.   **b** go to school.   **c** stay home.

2 You shouldn't
  a run around.   **b** rest.   **c** drink water.

3 You shouldn't
  a go to a doctor.   **b** eat candy.   **c** take care of yourself.

Story

5 **Read. Then answer the questions.**

You're Hurt!

"Oh, no!"

"Oh, no! You have a cut."

"What? I..."

"You should see the school nurse! You should put a bandage on that."

"But Sam..."

1 What are Sam and Christina doing?

_____

2 Who does Sam think Christina should see?

_____

3 What does Sam think Christina should do?

_____

6 **Read and complete the sentences.**

| bandage | run | nurse | rest |

"I fell and cut my knee. Ouch!"

You should <u>see the school nurse.</u>

_____.

_____.

You shouldn't _____.

THINK BIG

Look at 5 again. What happens next in the story? Write.

_____

_____

How did I do? ☆☆☆☆☆

74
7 Listen and match.

1 Michael's dad thinks he should   a headache.

2 Vicky should   b take better care of herself.

3 Jinsoo has a bad   c takes good care of himself.

4 Emily's big sister should   d have some crackers.

5 Dennis's grandfather   e allergies.

6 Sally has   f lie down and rest.

8 Read and circle T for true or F for false.

Nurse: What's the matter, Jessica?
Jessica: I don't feel good.
Nurse: Let me check you out.
Jessica: My tooth hurts.
Nurse: Oh! You should take some medicine.
Jessica: OK. That's all?
Nurse: No, you should see a dentist.

1 Jessica feels great.   T   F

2 Jessica has a stomachache.   T   F

3 Jessica has a toothache.   T   F

4 The nurse thinks Jessica is sick.   T   F

5 Jessica should go to the dentist.   T   F

How did I do? ☆ ☆ ☆ ☆ ☆

Grammar

I		I	
You		You	
He/She	**should** eat healthy foods.	He/She	**shouldn't** stay up late.
We		We	
They		They	

I		**myself.**
You		**yourself.**
He/She	should take care of	**himself/herself.**
We		**ourselves.**
They		**themselves.**

9 **Circle the correct words.**

1 I **should / shouldn't** eat more vegetables.

2 You **should / shouldn't** drink so much soda.

3 He **should / shouldn't** exercise every day.

4 We **should / shouldn't** stay up late.

5 They **should / shouldn't** eat healthy food.

10 **Read and ✓ the correct word.**

1 I go to bed late and eat potato chips. I should take better care of _____.

☐ myself ☐ yourself ☐ herself

2 You never eat fruit. You should take better care of _____.

☐ myself ☐ yourself ☐ ourselves

3 She doesn't exercise. She should take better care of _____.

☐ himself ☐ themselves ☐ herself

How did I do? ☆☆☆☆☆

11 **Write should or shouldn't.**

1 **Joe:** I have a headache.

   Doctor: You _____should_____ take some medicine.

2 **Mom:** My daughter has a sore throat.

   Doctor: She _____ take care of herself.

3 **Tim:** I'm really tired.

   Doctor: You _____ stay up so late.

4 **Dad:** My children have allergies.

   Doctor: They _____ stay inside and take medicine.

5 **Mom:** My son has a fever.

   Doctor: He _____ go to school.

6 **Sonya:** I like to watch TV for hours every day.

   Doctor: You _____ watch so much TV.

12 **Read the problems and write advice. Use should or shouldn't.**

1 I have a cough and a sore throat.

   _____

2 My brother has a cut on his leg.

   _____

3 My friends don't eat vegetables.

   _____

4 I have a stomachache.

   _____

5 I have a fever.

   _____

13 Listen, read, and complete. When should we use tissues?

clean	dirty water	diseases	enemies
microscope	Protect	spread	toothbrush

1 About Germs

We try to stay healthy, but there are tiny ¹_____ all around us called germs. They're always there, but we can only see them with a ²_____. Unfortunately, they can cause ³_____.

2 Where Are Germs?

They are everywhere. In the air, on old food, in ⁴_____, and on everything we touch with our dirty hands: the sink, the bathtub, our ⁵_____, the TV remote control, and our computer keyboards.

Germs

3 Kinds of Germs

There isn't just one kind of germ, there are at least four. Each one is a little different. The main ones are bacteria, viruses, fungi, and protozoa.

4 How Do We ⁶_____ Ourselves?

We can wash our hands often and keep the house ⁷_____. When we have a cold or a cough, we should use tissues. Also, we should stay at home, so our germs don't ⁸_____.

14 Look at 13. Answer the questions.

1 How many kinds of germs are there? _____

2 Can germs make us sick? _____

3 Write three ways we can stay away from germs. _____

_____

How did I do? ☆ ☆ ☆ ☆ ☆

15 **Match. Look at page 50 of your Student's Book.**

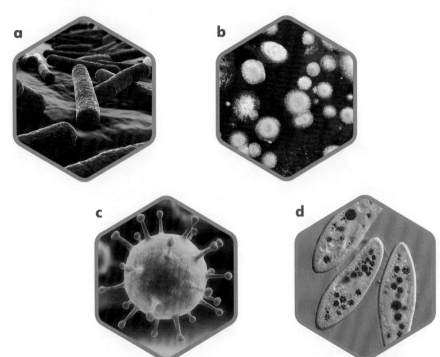

1 virus

2 bacteria

3 fungi

4 protozoa

16 **Write germs 1–4 from 15 next to the information. Use the text on page 50 of your Student's Book.**

1 They grow on old food. _____ . _____

2 They live in dirty water. _____

3 It's in the air and gives us coughs and colds. _____

4 The disease malaria comes from this. _____

5 They're sometimes good and help us digest food. _____

6 It can spread quickly through sneezes. _____

How did I do? ☆ ☆ ☆ ☆ ☆

17 Read and ✓.

Ginger is used around the world as a home remedy for many different problems. For example, many people take it when they have a stomachache. In Japan, mothers give their children ginger tea with sugar when they have a cough or a cold. In Europe, people drink it in hot water with honey and lemon to help with sore throats.

Garlic is also a common home remedy. In Spain, people add it to their tea to help with colds and coughs. Some Native Americans put it on bee stings. It helps stop the sting from hurting.

Cinnamon is another common home remedy. Many people use it for colds, but did you know you can also use it to help with a toothache? Just mix some with honey and put it on the sore tooth. This not only helps the tooth hurt less, but also tastes delicious.

	bee sting	cold	sore throat	stomachache	toothache
ginger					
garlic					
cinnamon					

18 Read and match.

1 A relaxing drink. Sometimes it's a home remedy for sore throats.

2 When you rub someone to help them relax.

3 Sleep is the best way to do this.

4 When you have a fever, this makes your body feel cooler.

5 You feel this before exams and during difficult times.

a rest

b herbal tea

c massage

d stress

e vinegar

How did I do? ☆ ☆ ☆ ☆ ☆

19 **Are commas used correctly? Read and ✓ or ✗.**

1 **a** First, I eat a healthy breakfast. Then I go swimming.
 b First I eat a healthy breakfast. Then, I go swimming.

2 **a** You should drink some tea take some medicine and sleep.
 b You should drink some tea, take some medicine, and sleep.

3 **a** I take good care of myself.
 She takes good care of herself too.
 b I take good care of myself.
 She takes good care of herself, too.

20 **Add commas in the correct places.**

1 I get a lot of rest drink water exercise and eat fruit.

2 I don't eat cookies cake chocolate or candy.

3 First I should eat a healthy dinner. Then I should do my homework. Finally I should go
 to bed.

4 The four kinds of germs are bacteria fungi protozoa and viruses.

5 You should drink some tea. You should take some medicine too.

21 **Write advice. Remember to use commas.**

1 I want to eat a healthy lunch. What should I eat?

_____

_____

2 I want to be healthy and exercise. What should I do?

_____

_____

3 I have a stomachache and a fever. What should I do?

_____

_____

22 **Read and circle kn and wr.**

knee   breakfast   wrist

knight   write   wrong

know   knock   right

now   wrap

23 **Underline the words with kn and wr. Then read aloud.**

1   The knight knows how to write.

2   He wraps his knee and knots the rope.

24 **Connect the letters. Then write.**

1   kn   eck   a   _ _ _ _ _

2   wr   ock   b   _ _ _ _ _

25 **Listen and write.**
82

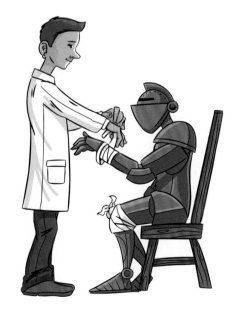

What's wrong, ¹ _____,wrong?

The ² _____ knocked his

Knee, knee, knee,

And his wrist, wrist, ³ _____.

I ⁴ _____! Wrap his knee

And ⁵ _____ his wrist!

How did I do? ☆☆☆☆☆

26 **Read and match.**

1 We have to

2 Germs make

3 Bacteria is

4 Germs get into

a one kind of germ.

b many places.

c protect ourselves from germs.

d a kind of poison called a toxin.

27 **Read and circle the correct words.**

1 She stays up late every night. She should take better care of **himself** / **herself**.

2 They take good care of **themselves** / **ourselves**. They exercise every morning.

3 I eat a lot of chips. I should take better care of **myself** / **yourself**.

4 You always eat a healthy lunch. You take good care of **yourself** / **ourselves**.

28 **Look and complete the sentences. Use words from the box and should or shouldn't.**

| allergies | cut | fever | headache | sore throat | stomachache |

1 She has a _____. She _____ drink water and rest.

2 He has a _____. He _____ talk too much.

3 She has a _____. She _____ go to school.

4 He has a _____. He _____ eat so much candy.

5 She has _____. She _____ go outside.

6 He has a _____. He _____ take better care of himself.

How did I do? ☆☆☆☆☆

5 Weird and Wild Animals

Vocabulary

1 Look and write. Then match.

> angler fish   coconut crabs   tarsiers   Tasmanian devils   volcano rabbits

1 _____

a They have long teeth, and they live in oceans all over the world. We don't know how many there are.

2 _____

b They have big eyes and brown fur. They live in Southeast Asia, but we don't know their population.

3 _____

c They have a population of more than 100,000, and they live on islands in the Pacific Ocean. They're orange and brown.

4 _____

d They have gray fur, and they live on volcanoes in Mexico. They have a population of between 2,000 and 12,000.

5 _____

e They have black and white fur. They have a population of between 10,000 and 25,000, and you can find them in Tasmania.

88
2 Listen and write. Then draw.

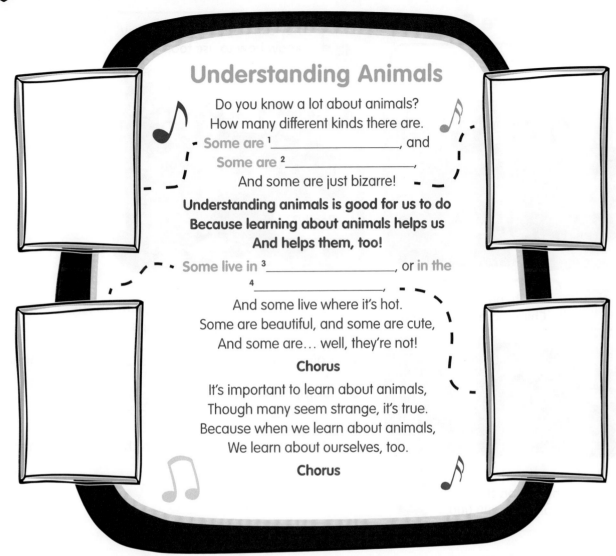

Understanding Animals

Do you know a lot about animals?
How many different kinds there are.
Some are ¹_____, and
Some are ²_____,
And some are just bizarre!

Understanding animals is good for us to do
Because learning about animals helps us
And helps them, too!

Some live in ³_____, or in the
⁴_____,
And some live where it's hot.
Some are beautiful, and some are cute,
And some are… well, they're not!

Chorus

It's important to learn about animals,
Though many seem strange, it's true.
Because when we learn about animals,
We learn about ourselves, too.

Chorus

3 Complete the chart. Use the names of animals you know.

big	small	live in trees	live in the ocean

How did I do? ☆☆☆☆☆

4 Read. Then complete the sentences.

Chimps Are Smart!

Wow! Chimpanzees are amazing animals. They can talk to each other!

They can climb trees, and they know how to use tools, too!

Really?

Oh, no! That's sad. Chimps are endangered.

A hundred years ago there were more than one million chimps. But now there are only 200,000.

1 Christina is watching a program about _____, or chimps.

2 Chimps are smart and _____ animals.

3 Chimps can _____ trees and _____ to each other.

4 There aren't many chimps in the wild – they're _____.

5 Answer about you.

1 Can you do any of the things that chimps can do?

_____

2 Do you like chimps? Why/Why not?

_____

THINK BIG

Chimps use tools to get food. What tools do you use to...

a cook/eat food? _____

b do your homework? _____

c stay clean? _____

How did I do?

92

6 **Listen and complete the sentences.**

1 Bumblebee _____ are endangered.
   There are only _____ left. Farmers
   burn trees where they live.

2 There are only about _____ tigers left
   in the world. There were more tigers, but people kill
   them for their _____ and to make medicine.

3 Red _____ come from China and the Himalayas. They are
   _____ because people are cutting down the trees where they live.

4 There were over 50,000 Egyptian _____ in the wild. Now there are only
   about 7,500 because people keep them as _____.

5 Mexican walking _____ are almost extinct. They live in streams and ponds,
   but their _____ are polluted.

200	fur
3,000	habitats
bats	pandas
endangered	pets
fish	tortoises

7 **Write the animal's name. Why is each animal endangered? Match.**

a

1 _____

2 _____

b

c

3 _____

d

4 _____

Grammar

> **How many** chimpanzees were there 100 years ago?
>
> There **were** more than one million. But now there **are** only about 200,000.

8 Read the chart. Then complete the dialogs.

		There were . . .	There are . . .
	Komodo dragon	How many? more than 20,000 When? fifty years ago	How many? fewer than 5,000 When? now
	Andean condor	How many? many When? in the past	How many? a few thousand When? now
	volcano rabbit	How many? 1,000 When? fifty years ago	How many? probably a few hundred When? now
	Tasmanian devil	How many? 100,000 When? twenty-five years ago	How many? 20,000 When? now

1 **A:** ___How many___ (volcano rabbits) ___were there___ fifty years ago?

   B: ___There were___ 1,000. Now ___there are___ probably a few hundred.

2 **A:** _____ (_____) _____ in the past?

   B: _____ many. Now _____ only a few thousand.

3 **A:** _____ (_____) _____ fifty years ago?

   B: _____ more than 20,000. Now _____ fewer than 5,000.

4 **A:** _____ (_____) _____ twenty-five years ago?

   B: _____ 100,000. Now _____ 20,000.

How did I do? ☆ ☆ ☆ ☆ ☆

> **Why** are chimpanzees endangered? | They're endangered **because** people are moving into their habitat.

9 Why are they endangered? Follow each maze. Then complete the dialogs.

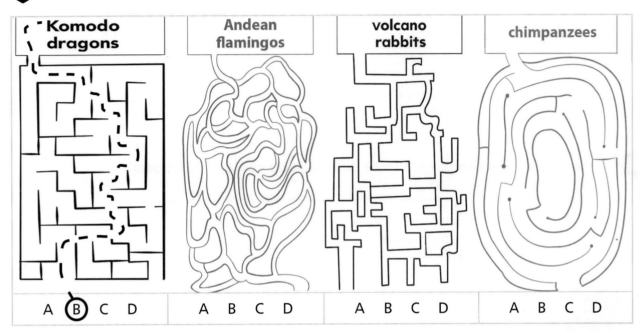

Komodo dragons	Andean flamingos	volcano rabbits	chimpanzees
A (B) C D	A B C D	A B C D	A B C D

A = There is too much pollution.   C = People are moving into their habitat.
B = People are killing them.   D = They are getting sick and dying.

1 **A:** _____Why_____ are Komodo dragons endangered?

   B: They're endangered ____because____ (people are killing them).

2 **A:** _____ are Andean flamingos endangered?

   B: They're endangered _____ ( ).

3 **A:** _____ are volcano rabbits endangered?

   B: They're endangered _____ ( ).

4 **A:** _____ are chimpanzees endangered?

   B: They're endangered _____ ( ).

How did I do? ☆☆☆☆☆

10 **Read and choose the correct answer.**

1 A _____ hunts and kills animals to eat.
   a predator   **b** trap

2 When there are only a few of one type of animal, they're _____.
   a extinct   **b** endangered

3 People hunt red pandas for their _____.
   a fur   **b** hair

4 Animals are not safe from diseases or hunting when they live in the _____.
   a world   **b** wild

11 94 **Listen, read, and complete. Which animals do people keep as pets?**

> bumblebee   habitats   pandas   predators
> salamander   tortoise   wild

Status: Endangered

You can sometimes find ¹_____ bats in caves in the forests of Myanmar and Thailand. However, there are now fewer than 6,000 left in the ²_____ because farmers burn the trees where they live.

Most red ³_____ live in China and the Himalayas, and they eat leaves. They hide in trees covered in red moss so that ⁴_____ don't see their beautiful red fur. They're endangered – there are now fewer than 10,000 – because people are destroying the bamboo forests.

The Egyptian ⁵_____ is very small – it's only 10 centimeters long. That makes it the smallest of its kind in the world. Many scientists believe there are only 7,500 left in the wild now because people keep them as pets.

The Mexican walking fish lives on land and in water. It's called a fish, but it's really a type of ⁶_____, with small legs. Unfortunately, this strange fish is almost extinct. It lives in streams and ponds, but now its ⁷_____ are mostly polluted.

How did I do? ☆☆☆☆☆

12 Look at 11. Then circle T for true or F for false.

1 Farmers protect bumblebee bats.   T   F

2 The Egyptian tortoise is the smallest in the world.   T   F

3 Red pandas hide in trees.   T   F

4 The Mexican walking fish lives in the forest.   T   F

13 Complete the sentences.

| caves   extinct   polluted   pond   Scientists |

1 Bumbleebee bats live in _____ because they like the dark.

2 The Mexican walking fish is nearly _____. There are fewer than 1,000 left.

3 Rivers in towns and cities are often _____. You can't swim in them.

4 _____ try to protect endangered species.

5 There is a large _____ at the end of our yard with small fish and frogs.

14 Which animal would you like as a pet? Explain.

_____

_____

_____

_____

_____

15 **Read and complete.**

| breathe | giants | lizard | mythical |
| myths | real | scary | wings |

There's only one ¹_____ dragon. It's the Komodo dragon, and it lives on a tiny Indonesian island. Actually, it isn't a dragon, it's a very large ²_____. All other dragons are ³_____ creatures. That means they exist only in ⁴_____ or fairy stories.

Some dragon tales are very frightening – they tell us about ⁵_____ beasts. These beasts are very large – they're ⁶_____ of the sky. They have enormous ⁷_____, and they ⁸_____ fire.

16 **Find four pairs of synonyms and three pairs of antonyms.**

1	tale		**a**	story
2	giant		**b**	frightening
3	humans		**c**	evil
4	good		**d**	south
5	scary		**e**	mythical
6	real		**f**	people
7	north		**g**	very big

How did I do? ☆ ☆ ☆ ☆ ☆

17 **Look and match.**

1 exclamation point	**!**	**?**
2 period		
3 question mark	**.**	

18 **Put a period, a question mark, or an exclamation point.**

1 How many chimps were there 100 years ago_____

2 Coconut crabs live on islands in the Pacific Ocean_____

3 Wow_____ That frog is so amazing_____

4 Why are chimps endangered_____

5 Look_____ A dragon_____

6 They have a population of 100,000_____

19 **Write sentences. Use a period, a question mark, or an exclamation point.**

1
angler fish

_____

_____

2
tigers

_____

_____

3
Tasmanian devils

_____

_____

4
volcano rabbits

_____

_____

5
Andean condors

_____

_____

6
black rhinos

_____

_____

How did I do? ☆☆☆☆☆

20 **Read and circle ph and wh.**

phone   panda   wheel

phantom

photo   white   wild

whale

dolphin   fish   wheat

21 **Underline the words with ph and wh. Then read aloud.**

1 When was the white elephant in the wheat?

2 I took a photo with my phone of a whale and a dolphin.

22 **Connect the letters. Then write.**

1 ph   en   **a** __ __ __ __

2 wh   one   **b** __ __ __ __ __

23 **Listen and write.**

The phantom has a ¹ _____
On his ² _____
Of a ³ _____ wheel
And some ⁴ _____ .

How did I do? ☆ ☆ ☆ ☆ ☆

24 **Unscramble and complete the sentences.**

1 Some scientists believe there are fewer than 7,500 Egyptian tortoises left in the
_____. (ldiw)

2 Most bumblebee bats live in _____ in Thailand. (vesac)

3 Red _____ eat bamboo leaves. (dpnasa)

4 Most scientists believe that the Mexican walking fish is almost _____. (cnetxit)

25 **Complete the dialogs with words from the box.**

because   chimpanzees   habitat   How many
tarsiers   There are   There were

1

A: Why are _____ endangered?

B: They're endangered _____ people are
destroying their _____.

2

A: _____ Andean condors are there now?

B: _____ only about 10,000 left in
the wild.

3

A: How many _____ were there a hundred
years ago?

B: _____ more than a million.

26 **Answer about you.**

Do you think it's important to help endangered animals? Why/Why not?

_____

_____

_____

_____

How did I do? ☆☆☆☆☆

Life Long Ago

Vocabulary

1 **Read and write the letters. Then trace the path.**

L	drive cars	**L**	wash clothes in a washing machine
I	traveled by horse and buggy	**G**	cooked on a coal stove
G	had oil lamps	**A**	have electric lights
E	listened to the radio	**F**	listen to an MP3 player
N	cook in a microwave	**O**	have a cell phone
O	washed clothes by hand	**!**	had a phone with an operator

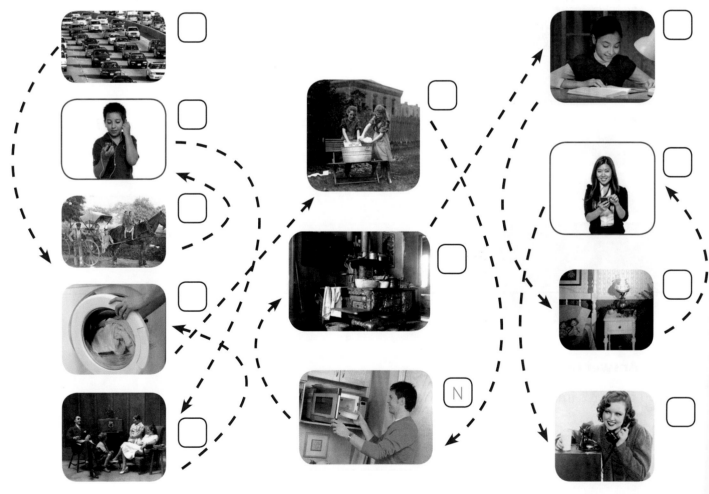

2 **Look at the letters in 1. Follow the path and write the letters. What do they spell?**

_____ _____ _____

Song

106

3 **Listen and match.**

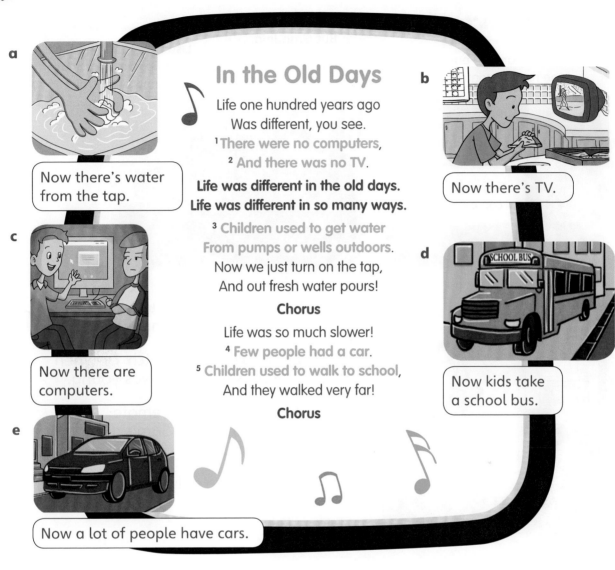

a

Now there's water from the tap.

c

Now there are computers.

e

Now a lot of people have cars.

In the Old Days

Life one hundred years ago
Was different, you see.
[1] There were no computers,
[2] And there was no TV.

Life was different in the old days.
Life was different in so many ways.

[3] Children used to get water
From pumps or wells outdoors.
Now we just turn on the tap,
And out fresh water pours!

Chorus

Life was so much slower!
[4] Few people had a car.
[5] Children used to walk to school,
And they walked very far!

Chorus

b

Now there's TV.

d

Now kids take a school bus.

4 **Write about now and long ago.**

Now

Long Ago

_____   _____

_____   _____

_____   _____

_____   _____

_____   _____

_____   _____

How did I do? ☆☆☆☆☆

Story

5 **Read. Then circle T for true or F for false.**

Life Was Nicer Then

1 Grandma is too lazy to change the channel. **T** **F**

2 People didn't watch TV when Sam's grandma was young. **T** **F**

3 There were no remote controls when Sam's grandma was a child. **T** **F**

4 There are only three channels now. **T** **F**

THINK BIG

What did your grandma have when she was a child?
Read and ✓ or ✗. Then write.

computer ☐ phone ☐ washing machine ☐ microwave ☐

car ☐ bike ☐ TV remote control ☐ books ☐ radio ☐

My grandma had _____

_____.

She didn't have _____

_____.

How did I do? ☆☆☆☆☆

6 Write the now and long ago activities.

> have electric lights   use a computer   wash clothes in a washing machine
> had oil lamps   washed clothes by hand   wrote letters by hand

a _washed clothes by hand_

b _____

c _____

d _____

e _____

f _____

7 Look at 6. Listen and number the pictures in the order you hear them.

How did I do? ☆☆☆☆☆

Grammar

Did people **have** cars in 1950?	Yes, they **did**.
Did people **have** cars in 1900?	No, they **didn't**. They traveled by horse and buggy or by train.

8   **Read and complete the answers. Use did or didn't.**

1 **A:** Did your grandmother have a TV when she was young?

   B: _____Yes, she did_____, but the shows were all in black and white.

3 **A:** Did your grandfather play video games when he was a kid?

   B: _____ because people used to play other games then. They didn't have video games.

2 **A:** Did people have cars fifty years ago?

   B: _____, but they were different. They used more gas then.

4 **A:** Did people have washing machines long ago?

   B: _____. They washed their clothes by hand in those days.

9   **Complete the questions and answers.**

1

A: _____ Grandma _____ a dog when she was young?

B: _____, _____. She had a cute little dog.

2

A: _____ Mom _____ a cell phone in high school?

B: _____, _____. She used public pay phones.

3

A: _____ Dad _____ a computer in school?

B: _____, _____. He used a computer, but it was big and slow.

4

A: _____ Grandpa _____ emails when he was young?

B: _____, _____. He wrote letters, not emails.

How did I do? ☆ ☆ ☆ ☆ ☆

> Before TV, what **did** people **use to do** for entertainment at night?
>
> They **used to listen** to the radio.
> They **didn't use to listen** to an MP3 player.

10 **Complete the sentences.**

1   **A:** Before email, what _did people use to do_
    to communicate?

    B: They _used to write letters_ .

2   **A:** Before washing machines, what _____
    to wash clothes?

    B: They _____ .

3   **A:** Before electricity, what _____
    for light?

    B: They _____ .

4   **A:** Before TV, what _____
    for entertainment?

    B: They _____ .

11 **Answer about you.**

1   Before you could read, what did you use to do?

    _____

2   Before you could ride a bike, what did you use to do?

    _____

12 **Look in your house. What used to be different?**

We used to have an old and slow computer. Now we have a new one.

1   _____

2   _____

3   _____

How did I do? ☆ ☆ ☆ ☆ ☆

13 Complete the sentences.

| distance   engine   average speed   number of   per hour |

1 The _____ of a modern plane is about 885 km per hour.

2 Planes are a great way to travel a long _____ because they're fast.

3 The average man can walk at a speed of 5 km _____.

4 Bad traffic means there is a large _____ cars on the roads.

5 A car can't travel without an _____.

112

14 Listen, read, and circle. How did people travel before cars?

What did people do before they had cars? Well, lucky people used to travel by horse and buggy. And unlucky people walked. Both forms of travel were **¹uncomfortable / slow**, but the horse and buggy was a little more comfortable. It had an average speed of 8 kilometers (km) per hour. Historians believe people didn't travel for longer than about three hours per day, probably because it was very **²tiring / expensive**.

Horse and Buggy

Model T

Mr. Henry Ford built the first Model T, or "Tin Lizzie", in 1908. It changed the way we travel. For the first time, a car was not a luxury. The car became a **³popular / cheap** means of transport, and everybody with a job and some money could buy one. The Model T had an average speed of 40 km per hour. Suddenly, there were more vehicles on the roads, and it was more **⁴exciting / dangerous**.

Today, there are many different **⁵modern / new** cars. Some are for racing, some are luxury cars, and some are family cars. They're all faster than they used to be. An average family car can travel at a speed of more than 150 km per hour. But they never do. The average speed of modern cars is 90 km per hour. This is because there are strict speed limits, and there is a lot of **⁶noise / traffic**.

Modern Car

How did I do? ☆☆☆☆☆

15   **Look at 14. Read and answer.**

1   How many hours did people travel each day with a horse and buggy?

_____

2   Who could buy a Model T?

_____

3   What types of cars can we find today?

_____

4   Today, cars can't travel fast. Why not?

_____

16   **Look at the average speeds in 14 and solve the equations.**

1   A horse and buggy travels for 10 hours. How far does it travel?

_____ x _____ = _____ km
_{average speed}   _{number of hours}   _{distance travelled}

2   A Model T travels for 6 hours. How far does it travel?

_____ x _____ = _____ km

3   A horse and buggy travels for 8 hours. How far does it travel?

_____ x _____ = _____ km

4   A modern car travels for 2 hours. How far does it travel?

_____ x _____ = _____ km

5   A Model T travels for 7 hours. How far does it travel?

_____ x _____ = _____ km

6   A modern car travels for 3 hours. How far does it travel?

_____ x _____ = _____ km

How did I do?   ☆☆☆☆☆

17   Read. Then ✓.

The Hmong

The Hmong are hill people. They live in the mountains of Southeast Asia. They have their own way of life and their own language. You won't find much modern technology in a traditional Hmong village because people there live the way their ancestors did 2,000 years ago.

The Maasai

The Maasai of Kenya are a nomadic tribe. This means they move from place to place and make new homes each time. Their villages don't have running water or electricity, so they can't use modern technology in their homes.

The Koryak

The Koryak live in the northern part of Russia's Pacific coast. Their land is Arctic tundra, and it's very cold. For food, they herd reindeer and catch fish. They also make some of their clothes. They wear warm hats made of reindeer skins to protect them from the freezing temperatures.

		The Hmong	The Koryak	The Maasai
1	They live in Russia.			
2	They move from place to place.			
3	They live in Southeast Asia.			
4	They wear reindeer skin hats.			
5	They live in Kenya.			
6	They live like people did 2,000 years ago.			

18   **Look at 17. Choose words from the box to match the definitions.**

> ancestors   language   nomadic

1   We use this to speak and communicate.   _____

2   These are people from your family or tribe who aren't alive.   _____

3   These people don't stay in one place.   _____

How did I do? ☆☆☆☆☆

19 Put quotation marks in the correct places.

1 Did they watch movies in the 1920s? he asked.

2 I used to play soccer, said John.

3 Jamie yelled, I got a new bike!

4 Karen said, I wrote a letter last night.

20 Rewrite the sentences. Use said or asked and quotation marks.

¹How did people travel in 1905?

²Did you use to ride in a horse and buggy?

Ed   Mom

³They used to ride in a horse and buggy.

⁴I'm not that old!

1 _____

2 _____

3 _____

4 _____

21 Look and write what they are saying. Use asked or yelled and quotation marks.

1

2

22   **Read and circle ge and dge.**

fridge   cage   watched

traditional   washed   large

badge   edge   age

bridge   page

23   **Underline the words with ge and dge. Then read aloud.**

1   Look over the edge of the hedge. There's a bridge.

2   The boy's wearing a large badge and carrying a cage.

24   **Connect the letters. Then write.**

1   ca   dge   **a**   __ __ __ __ __

2   ba   ge   **b**   __ __ __ __ __ __

3   lar   ge   **c**   __ __ __ __ __

4   e   dge   **d**   __ __ __ __

 25   **Listen and write.**   *118*

There's a ¹ _____ fridge
On the ² _____ .
There's a large ³ _____
In the ⁴ _____ .

         How did I do? ☆ ☆ ☆ ☆ ☆

26 **Read and solve the equations.**

1 A school bus has an average speed of 60 kilometers per hour. How far does it travel in 3 hours?

_____ x _____ = _____ km

2 A bike has an average speed of 20 kilometers per hour. How far does it travel in 6 hours?

_____ x _____ = _____ km

27 **Circle the correct words. Then answer the questions.**

1 **A:** **Did** / **Do** people have microwaves 100 years ago?

   B: _____

2 **A:** Did your city or town **had** / **have** cars ten years ago?

   B: _____

3 **A:** Did people **use to** / **used to** watch TV before electricity?

   B: _____

4 **A:** Did your dad **travel** / **traveled** to school by horse and buggy?

   B: _____

28 **Circle four things that didn't exist long ago. Write sentences with didn't use to in your notebook.**

29 **What were you and you family doing at these times yesterday?**

8 o'clock in the morning _____

12 o'clock, lunchtime _____

7 o'clock in the evening _____

How did I do? ☆☆☆☆☆

Sue's Path

1 Look at Units 4, 5, and 6. Choose words from the units. Write them in the charts.

2 Draw one path. Gather information and add your own.

HEALTH PROBLEMS

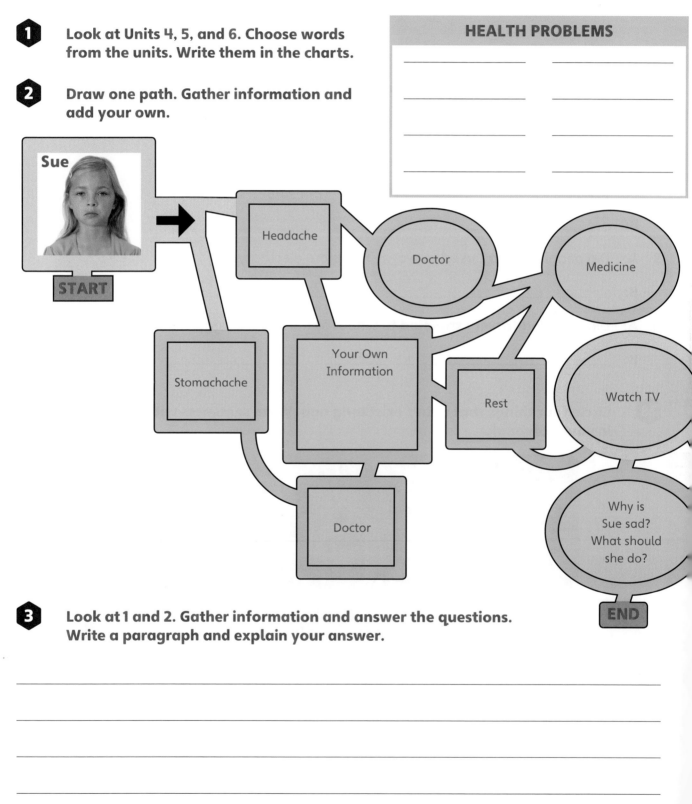

3 Look at 1 and 2. Gather information and answer the questions. Write a paragraph and explain your answer.

ENDANGERED ANIMALS	TECHNOLOGY NOW
_____	_____
_____	_____
_____	_____
_____	_____

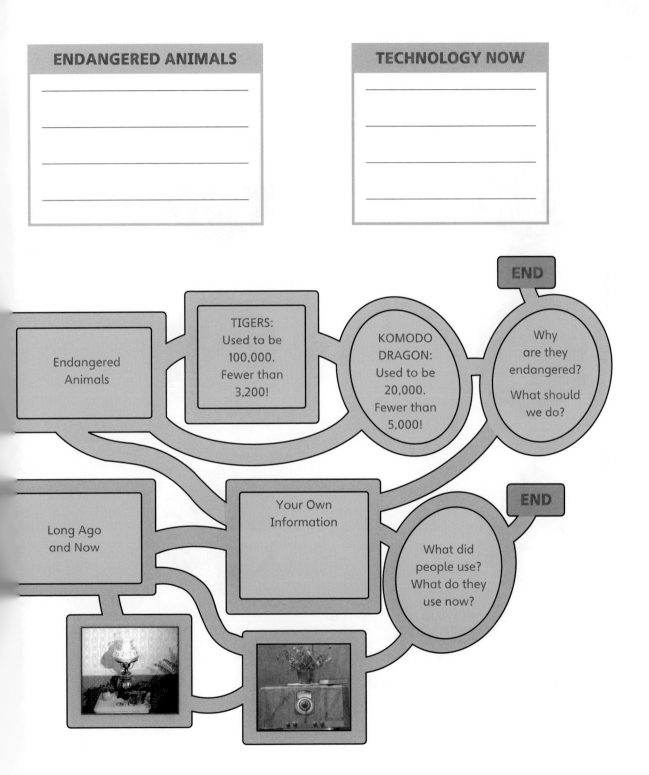

Endangered Animals

TIGERS:
Used to be 100,000.
Fewer than 3,200!

KOMODO DRAGON:
Used to be 20,000.
Fewer than 5,000!

Why are they endangered?
What should we do?

END

Long Ago and Now

Your Own Information

What did people use? What do they use now?

END

Special Days

Vocabulary

 1 **Look and write the special days.**

1 _____

2 _____

3 _____

4 _____

5 _____

6 _____

2 **Read and circle T for true or F for false.**

1 My parents' anniversary is celebrated by my mom and dad.   T   F

2 New Year's Day is before New Year's Eve.   T   F

3 On Valentine's Day, people give flowers to their loved ones.   T   F

4 There is a parade on Earth Day.   T   F

3 Listen and write. Use the words from the box.

What Do We Do on Special Days?

This ¹_____ is a special day –
The last day of the year.
We're ²_____ stay up very late.
At midnight, we're going to cheer!

Special days are cool. Special days are fun.
Special days bring special treats for everyone!

On the first of ³_____,
We are going to say,
"Happy New Year!" to everyone
Because it's ⁴_____.

Chorus

There are a lot of special days,
And this one is a treat.
We're going to
Have ⁵_____
And ⁶_____,
And delicious food to eat!

Chorus

fireworks
Friday
going to
January
New Year's Day
parades

4 Look at 3 and ✓ the correct answers.

1 This Friday is…

⬜ December 30th.   ⬜ December 31st.   ⬜ January 1st.

2 They are going to cheer…

⬜ at lunchtime.   ⬜ in the afternoon.   ⬜ at midnight.

3 On New Year's Eve, they…

⬜ stay up late.   ⬜ go to bed early.   ⬜ sleep late.

5 Read. Then answer the questions.

The Anniversary Party

What are you doing, Sam?

Well, tomorrow is June 10th. I'm making a cake for your anniversary!

We're going to have dinner at Antonio's, your favorite restaurant.

Oh... yes, right!

That's very kind of you!

Yes, very nice, but...

Our anniversary is on July 10th, not June 10th!

1 Why is Sam planning a celebration?

_____

2 Where are they going to go?

_____

3 What's the problem?

_____

6 Write about you and your family.

1 My birthday is on _____ .

2 My mom's birthday is on _____ .

3 My dad's birthday is on _____ .

4 My parents' wedding anniversary is on _____ .

THINK BIG

Think and write. What do you think Sam's parents are going to say next?

_____   _____

How did I do? ☆ ☆ ☆ ☆ ☆

130

7 Listen and match.

Dad's birthday

sister's birthday

go to a parade

Dad's party/give presents

FEBRUARY

SUNDAY	MONDAY	TUESDAY	WEDNESDAY	THURSDAY	FRIDAY	SATURDAY
					1	2
3	4	5	6	7	8	9
10	**11**	**12**	**13**	**14**	**15**	**16**
17	18	19	20	21	22	23
24	25	26	27	28		

Mom's special dinner

sister's party

Grandparents' anniversary

Mom's birthday

Valentine's Day

8 Look at the calendar in 7. Write the dates and special days.

1 _____

_____

2 _____

_____

3 _____

_____

Grammar

When **are**	you	**going to have** the party?	I	**am going to have** it on Monday.
			We	**are going to have** it on Monday.
			They	
When **is**	he/she	**going to visit** Grandma?	He/She	**is going to visit** her next month.

9 Answer the questions about Sarah's calendar.

MAY

Sun	Mon	Tue	Wed	Thu	Fri	Sat
1	2	3 today	4	5	6	7 birthday party
8	9	10	11 parents' anniversary	12	13	14 sister visits friend
15	16	17	18 watch parade	19	20	21 watch fireworks
22	23	24	25	26	27 Uncle Joe visits	28
29	30	31				

1   When is Sarah going to have her birthday party?

<u>She is going to have it on Saturday, the seventh.</u>

2   When are her parents going to celebrate their anniversary?

_____

3   When is her sister going to visit her friend?

_____

4   Is she going to watch the parade on the 17th?

_____

5   Are they going to watch the fireworks on Sunday?

_____

How did I do? ☆ ☆ ☆ ☆ ☆

Are you/they going to visit Grandma **on the ninth**?	Yes, **on the ninth**.
Is he/she going to visit Grandma **on the fifth**?	No, **on the ninth**.

10 **Read and cross out the letters. Use the remaining letters to write the special days.**

1 Cross out the first, third, fifth, ninth, tenth, twelfth, and fourteenth letters.

~~E~~ E ~~X~~ A ~~B~~ R T H ~~X~~ ~~N~~ D ~~O~~ A ~~M~~ Y

<u>E</u> <u>A</u> <u>R</u> <u>T</u> <u>H</u>　<u>D</u> <u>A</u> <u>Y</u>

2 Cross out the first, third, seventh, tenth, thirteenth, sixteenth, seventeenth, and twentieth letters.

B V I A L E R N T H I N P E S Y N D A O Y

___ ___ ___ ___ ___ ___ ___ ___ , ___ ___ ___ ___

3 Cross out the second, fourth, sixth, seventh, ninth, eleventh, sixteenth, seventeenth, and nineteenth letters.

N A E H W P V Y I E N A R S D E V A E Y

___ ___ ___ ___ ___ ___ ___ , ___ ___ ___ ___

11 **Read and write the answer.**

Sam has to go to the dentist on the ninth of March. It is a regular checkup and cleaning. On the fifteenth of March, he is going to have his birthday party. His cousins can't come. So on the twentieth of March, he is going to visit his cousins. They are going to go to the movies.

1 When is Sam going to celebrate his birthday?

_____

2 When is Sam going to visit his cousins?

_____

3 When is Sam going to have his teeth cleaned?

_____

How did I do? ☆☆☆☆☆

Content Connection | Geography

12 Listen, read, and circle. ⁽¹³³⁾

Holi, The Festival of Colors

This festival takes place every year to **¹watch / celebrate** the end of winter and the arrival of spring. It's celebrated in India, Nepal, and other places. It's probably the most colorful festival in the whole world. During Holi, people throw water and colored **²paper / powder**. People like to wear white clothes to Holi and watch them stain with all the different colors.

Tomatina, The Tomato Festival

Every year, on the last Wednesday of August, there is a **³clean / messy** festival in Buñol, Spain, where people throw tomatoes at each other. The festival started in 1945. There was no real reason for it. It was just good fun.

The Monkey Buffet

On the last weekend in November, the people of Lopburi, Thailand, invite hundreds of monkeys to a **⁴feast / fight** of peanuts, fruit, and vegetables. People come from all over the world to watch the monkeys eat.

Quyllur Rit'i, The Festival of the Snow Star

It takes place every year in May or June on a **⁵volcano / glacier** in Peru. People celebrate with music and dancing for three days and nights, and the festival finishes with everyone carrying fire torches as they leave.

13 Look at 12. Complete the sentences and put a ✓ or a ✗.

attraction	clean	fight	takes place	torches

1 Every year in Buñol, there is a big tomato _____. ☐

2 In one festival in Thailand, people carry fire _____ down from the mountain. ☐

3 The Monkey Buffet Festival in Thailand isn't a popular tourist _____. ☐

4 It's very unusual to leave the Holi festival wearing _____ clothes. ☐

5 Quyllur Rit'i _____ only in June. ☐

How did I do? ☆☆☆☆☆

14 **Look at 12. Circle T for true and F for false.**

1 The Festival of Colors takes place in China.   T   F

2 People usually wear white clothes to Holi.   T   F

3 The Tomato Festival is celebrated in Spain.   T   F

4 People celebrate it to say "thank you" for all the tomatoes.   T   F

5 The Monkey Buffet takes place at the end of November
   in Thailand.   T   F

6 People celebrate the Festival of the Snow Star for three
   weeks in Peru.   T   F

15 **Answer the questions according to 12.**

1 Who are the guests at the Monkey Buffet?

_____

2 What foods do these guests enjoy?

_____

3 What makes the streets messy at the Tomato Festival?

_____

4 Why is it icy cold at the Festival of the Snow Star?

_____

5 Why does the colored powder stick to clothes at Holi?

_____

6 How does Quyllur Rit'i finish?

_____

How did I do? ☆ ☆ ☆ ☆ ☆

16 **Read about leap years.**

Leap Year

We usually say a year is 365 days long because that's about the time it takes for Earth to travel around the sun. It actually takes 365 days, 5 hours, 49 minutes, and 12 seconds. The extra 5 hours, 49 minutes, and 12 seconds add up to an extra day every four years on February 29th. This day is called leap day. Years with the extra day are called leap years. They can be divided evenly by four. For example, 2004, 2008, and 2012 were leap years.

17 **Answer the questions.**

1 How long does it take Earth to travel around the sun?

_____ days

_____ hours

_____ minutes

_____ seconds

2 How many days are there in a leap year? _____

18 **Solve these problems.**

1 Billy was born on February 29th, 2000. Write the next four years he can celebrate his birthday on February 29th.

_____ _____ _____ _____

2 It's February 29th, 2012. It's Jessi's birthday. Write the next four years she can celebrate her birthday on February 29th.

_____ _____ _____ _____

How did I do? ☆ ☆ ☆ ☆ ☆

19 **Read and complete the email. Use the words from the box.**

FROM   1 _____

TO   alex@bigenglish.com

SUBJECT   2 _____

3 _____ Alex,

Guess what! It's our street carnival next weekend. There are loads of things planned. I'm going to watch the parade because my sister's in it. She's going to wear special traditional clothes. Then I'm going to buy a present for my grandparents. It's their anniversary on June 13th.

I have to go. Write back soon!

4 _____

Simon

> Dear
> Next weekend
> simon@bigenglish.com
> Your friend,

20 **Write an email to a friend. Invite your friend to a celebration.**

> New Year's Day party   Midsummer's Day party

FROM

TO

SUBJECT

How did I do? ☆☆☆☆☆

21 Read and circle ue, u_e, and ure.

cute   glue   bridge

sponge   edge   picture

blue   cube

true   treasure

22 Underline the words with ue, u_e, and ure. Then read aloud.

1 This is a huge bottle of glue.

2 I drink pure water.

23 Connect the letters. Then write.

1 bl   ure   **a** __ __ __ __ __ __

2 c   ue   **b** __ __ __ __

3 nat   ube   **c** __ __ __ __

24  Listen and write.

Hi, ¹ _____.
Is it ² _____?
It's so ³ _____.
It's so ⁴ _____.
It's really ⁵ _____!
Is that a monster
In the ⁶ _____?

How did I do? ☆☆☆☆☆

Review

25 **Match. Then write sentences. Use going to.**

1 Dad/buy/a new camera

2 We/decorate/our classroom

3 Mom/buy/gifts

4 Kim/learn/all about computers

5 Tom/stay/at home

6 Jenny/eat/a big dinner

because

a run in a race tomorrow.

b take pictures of the Monkey Buffet.

c get a new laptop.

d watch his favorite TV program.

e meet our American cousins.

f have visitors from a school abroad.

1 _____

2 _____

3 _____

4 _____

5 _____

6 _____

26 **Look at the pictures. Answer the questions.**

FEBRUARY 14   MARCH 10   APRIL 22

1 When are they going to celebrate Earth Day?

_____

2 Is she going to have her birthday party on March 10th?

_____

3 Are they going to have a Valentine's Day party on February 9th?

_____

How did I do?

Hobbies

Vocabulary

1 **Draw the path. Connect the pictures. Then complete the question and answer.**

soccer player → painter → toy car collection → chess player →

coin collection → singer → video game player → shell collection →

doll collection → dancer → basketball player → writer

What _____?

_____

2 Listen and circle. Then answer the questions.

The Best and the Worst

Matthew collects toy cars.
He has one hundred seven.
But Pam's **¹ car / shell** collection is bigger.
She has three hundred
² eleven / ten!

Kay is good at games.
She's really good at **³ music / chess**.
But Paul is even better than Kay.
And Liz, well, she's the best!

What's your hobby, Bobby?
What do you like doing?
What's your hobby, Bobby?
What is fun for you?

Steve's a **⁴ great / terrible** singer.
Emma's worse than Steve.
But David's singing is the worst.
When he sings, people leave!

It's **⁵ bad / good** to have a hobby.
Some people have a few.
Even if you're not the best,
It still is fun to do!

Chorus

1 Who collects toy cars? _____

2 How many cars does Matthew have? _____

3 How many cars does Pam have? _____

4 Who is the best at games? _____

5 Is Steve a good singer? _____

6 Do people like listening to David's singing? _____

How did I do? ☆☆☆☆☆

3 Read. Then circle T for true and F for false.

The School Play

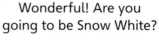

1 Christina's dad thinks the school play is boring.   **T   F**

2 He wants Christina to be Snow White.   **T   F**

3 Christina is a better singer than Lizzie.   **T   F**

4 Christina is taller than the other girls.   **T   F**

5 Christina is going to be a tree.   **T   F**

4 Write about you.

1 What character would you like to be in Snow White? Why?

_____

2 What are you good at?

_____

friendly   kind   nice
old   pretty

THINK BIG

Think about Snow White and the Evil Queen.
Who do you like better? Why? Use the words from the box.

_____

How did I do? ☆☆☆☆☆

Language in Action

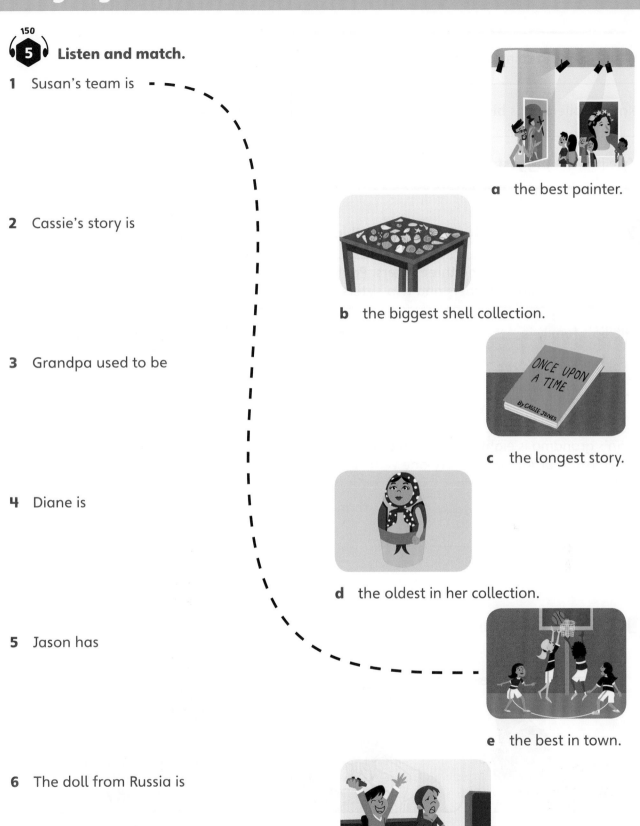

1   Susan's team is

2   Cassie's story is

3   Grandpa used to be

4   Diane is

5   Jason has

6   The doll from Russia is

a the best painter.

b the biggest shell collection.

c the longest story.

d the oldest in her collection.

e the best in town.

f the worst video game player.

How did I do? ⭐⭐⭐⭐⭐

| Chris has a **big** coin collection. |
| Katie's collection is **bigger** than Chris's collection. |
| Kyle has **the biggest** toy car collection. |

6 **Read. Then use a form of big, small, old, or young to complete each sentence.**

Philip has two brothers and three sisters. Pablo has three brothers and four sisters. Tony has two brothers and two sisters.

1 Philip's family is _____ than Tony's.

2 Pablo's family is the _____ of all.

3 Tony's family is _____.

Dean's grandma is eighty-six years old. Betty's grandma is seventy-four years old. Harriet's grandma is ninety-one years old.

4 Dean's grandma is _____ than Betty's grandma.

5 Betty's grandma is _____.

6 Harriet's grandma is the _____ of all.

7 **Look at the pictures. Write sentences using the words.**

| Pam | Sue | Mae |

1 _____ (older)

2 _____ (oldest)

How did I do? ☆☆☆☆☆

Laura is a **good** soccer player.	My brother's pictures are **bad**.
Steve is a **better** player **than** Laura.	My sister's pictures are **worse than** his.
Yoko is **the best** soccer player in the class.	My pictures are **the worst** of all.

8 Listen. Write and add the scores. Compare the scores and complete the sentences.

INDIVIDUAL SCORES

1 Tony's score

$7 + 7 + 8 = 22$

2 Molly's score

_____

3 Rob's score

_____

FINAL RESULTS

4 Tony is a good singer, but Rob is _____ .

5 Rob is a _____ singer _____ Tony.

6 Molly is _____ singer of all and the Next Big Star!

How did I do? ☆☆☆☆☆

9 **Match the words to the pictures.**

> **1** butterfly collection   **2** doll   **3** embroidery   **4** soccer

a  ☐   **b**  ☐   **c**  ☐   **d**  ☐

10 **Listen, read, and circle six mistakes. Then write the correct words.**

> china   drawing   employers   rocking   skirts   thread

Many sports today are not new. Soccer became popular in the 19th century. Back then, many soccer clubs were started by teachers so that the workers could play and stay fit. However, only male workers could play. Soccer was a man's sport. Both women and men played tennis and croquet. Sports for women were not easy because they had to wear long trousers. ¹_____ ²_____

Girls used to spend a lot of time at home. They did quiet activities with their hands. Many girls liked doing embroidery with a needle and rope. They used to embroider cushions and tablecloths. They also created beautiful pictures of flowers and birds with tiny colored stitches. ³_____

In the 19th century, the choice of toys for girls and boys was much smaller. Girls used to play with dolls and dollhouses. They had to be careful because the dolls were made of plastic. They could break quite easily. Jumping horses were also popular with boys and girls. Boys used to play with toy trains and railways. ⁴_____
⁵_____

People in the 19th century loved nature. One popular hobby was collecting and playing with butterflies. They caught the butterflies in nets then pinned them on boards to show their beautiful colors. ⁶_____

How did I do? ☆ ☆ ☆ ☆ ☆

11 **Look at 10. Read and circle.**

In the 19th century,

1 many men played soccer **in the park** / **at work**.

2 women used to **play with trains** / **croquet**.

3 women **went out** / **stayed at home** a lot.

4 women would embroider **tissues** / **cushions**.

5 girls' dolls **didn't break** / **broke** easily.

6 people **set free** / **showed** the insects they caught.

12 **Complete the sentences.**

> creativity   imagination   employers   sewing
> spare time   net   handmade

1 You use a needle and thread to do _____.

2 Most people do their hobbies in their _____.

3 This candy isn't from a store or a factory. It's _____.

4 Butterflies move quite slowly, so it's easy to catch them with a _____.

5 Children in the past had more _____ because they had to create their own games.

6 _____ started sports clubs so that the workers can have fun and stay fit.

7 Hobbies, both in the past and in the present, are a way for people to express their _____.

How did I do?

13 **Match to make phrases. Then complete the museum information.**

1 underwater   **a** sightings

2 UFO   **b** hair

3 locks of   **c** sculptures

Come in and leave your

_____

_____!

Come and read
information about

_____

_____!

Don't miss our

_____

_____!

14 **Read and match.**

1 A person who makes cups and plates.

2 This word describes ocean life.

3 A person who knows everything
about a subject.

4 The rocky homes of tiny underwater
animals – they're usually colorful.

5 Looking at things underwater with
a mask and breathing tube.

a corals

b snorkeling

c potter

d marine

e expert

How did I do? ☆ ☆ ☆ ☆ ☆

15 **Read and complete the informal letter. Use the words from the box.**

Beach View Hotel,
10 Pebble Lane,
Dorset,
DT1 XF2

August 12th, 2014
Dear
How are you?
Love,

1 _____

2 _____ Mia,

3 _____ I'm fine.

We're staying at the Beach View Hotel in Dorset, and it's great! I'm starting a shell collection. I got a lot yesterday. I went to the beach and saw them on the sand. The best one is beautiful and pink. I think it's my best shell yet. I'm having a great time on vacation. It's hot and sunny. Tomorrow we're going on a hike and maybe to the movies in the evening.

When I get home, I'll bring over my pictures and shells to show you.

4 _____

Beth

16 **Write an informal letter to a friend. Tell your friend about a hobby. Here are some ideas:**

a healthy hobby   a creative hobby   a hobby that helps you learn

_____

_____

_____

_____

_____

_____

_____

How did I do? ☆ ☆ ☆ ☆ ☆

17 Read and circle y and igh.

fly   try   light

high   my   picture

cute   true

sky   fight   night

18 Underline the words with y and igh. Then read aloud.

1 Birds fly high in the sky.

2 I watch the moon at night.

19 Connect the letters. Then write.

1 li   y   **a** __ __ __

2 m   ght   **b** __ __ __ __ __

3 fl   y   **c** __ __

159
20 Listen and write.

Let's ¹ _____,
Let's ² _____.
Let's ³ _____
And ⁴ _____
The ⁵ _____
At ⁶ _____!

How did I do? ☆ ☆ ☆ ☆ ☆

Review

21 Complete the dialogs with forms of bad, good, old and new.

1

A: Carol is _____ at chess.

B: Yes. But Henry is _____ Carol.

A: That's true. But I'm _____ of all.

2

A: Sean is a _____ singer.

B: I know! But Chris is _____ Sean.

A: Yes. But Brian is _____ singer of all.

3

A: Patty's Grandma is 90. That's really

_____.

B: Yes, but Marge's Grandma is _____ that. She's 98.

A: I know, and Randy's Grandma is _____ of all. She's over a hundred!

4

A: My dad got a car a few weeks ago. It's red and shiny and _____.

B: Oh yeah, well my dad got a car last week. It's _____ than your dad's car.

A: Well, maybe. But my friend's dad has a new car. It's the _____ of all. He got his car yesterday!

22 Answer about your family. Write complete sentences.

1 Who's the best singer? _____

2 Who's the worst singer? _____

3 Who's the best dancer? _____

4 Who's the worst dancer? _____

5 Who's the oldest person? _____

How did I do? ☆ ☆ ☆ ☆ ☆

9 Learning New Things

Vocabulary

1 **Do the crossword puzzle. Write the words below and in the boxes.**

Across →

1

sing like a rock star

2

draw ______ books

3

______

4

make a ______

Down ↓

5

______ a cake

6

build a ______

7

play the ______

8

______ like a hip-hop artist

2 **What things can you do? Write.**

______

______

______

166

3 Listen and write. Use the words from the box.

| bake | draw | learn | show | sing | skateboard | speak |

Learning Is Fun!

Do you know how to ¹_____?
It's so great. It's so cool!
I can ²_____ you how to do it
On Friday after school.
It's fun to learn new things,
Like how to ³_____
Or ⁴_____ or ⁵_____!
I wish I had a lot more free time.
I would try to ⁶_____ everything!
I'd like to learn to speak English.
"It's hard!" my friends all say.
But I think it's really interesting.
I'd like to ⁷_____ it well one day.

Chorus

Do you want
to learn English?

Yes!

4 What activities are amazing, dangerous, and difficult? Write.

1 I think it's amazing to _____

_____.

2 I think it's dangerous to _____

_____.

3 I think it's difficult to _____

_____.

5 **Read. Then circle.**

The Best in the Class

Isn't that boy in your class, Sam?

Oh, yes!

Hi, Jake! You're really good at playing the guitar.

Thanks!

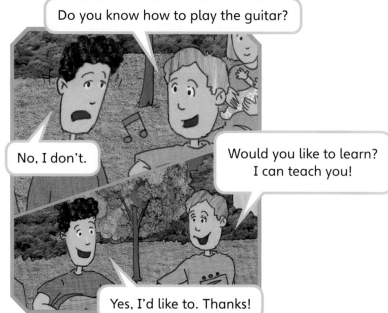

Do you know how to play the guitar?

No, I don't.

Would you like to learn? I can teach you!

Yes, I'd like to. Thanks!

Sam! I think it's terrible!

I think it's... um... interesting!

1 Jake is **in Sam's class** / **on the soccer team**.

2 He's good at playing the **piano** / **guitar**.

3 Sam **can** / **can't** play the guitar.

4 He **would** / **wouldn't** like to learn how to play the guitar.

5 Sam **is** / **isn't** very good at playing the guitar.

6 **Write about you.**

I'm good at _____.

I'd like to learn how to _____.

THINK BIG

What happens next in the story? Use these ideas or think of your own.

1 Sam practices every day and learns how to play the guitar very well.

2 Jake teaches Sam to play the guitar very well.

How did I do? ☆☆☆☆☆

7 **Listen. Then answer in complete sentences.**

1

Does Bobby want to learn how to skateboard? Why/Why not?

_____

_____

_____

2

Does Tommy want to learn how to dance hip-hop? Why/Why not?

_____

_____

_____

3

Does Diana want to learn how to play tennis? Why/Why not?

_____

_____

_____

4

Does Erik want to learn how to bake a cake? Why/Why not?

_____

_____

_____

How did I do? ☆ ☆ ☆ ☆ ☆

Grammar

Do you **know how to play** the piano?			Yes, I do. / No, I don't.	
What **would**	you	**like to learn**?	I'**d**	**like to learn how to play** the piano.
	he/she		He'**d**/She'**d**	
	they		They'**d**	

8 **Answer the questions in complete sentences.**

1 What would she like to learn?

_____

_____

2 What would he like to learn?

_____

_____

3 What would they like to learn?

_____

_____

4 What would she like to learn?

_____

_____

How did I do? ☆☆☆☆☆

What **do**	you	**think of** tennis?	I	**think** it's a lot of fun.
			We	
	they		They	
What **does**	he/she	**think of** ballet?	He/She	**thinks** it's boring.

9 **Look and answer the questions.**

1 What does he think of the movie?

_____

2 What does she think of the zoo?

_____

10 **Look at the school notice. Answer the questions in complete sentences.**

AFTER-SCHOOL CLASSES
WHAT WOULD YOU LIKE TO LEARN? SIGN UP HERE

CHESS
1 JOE
2 TOM
3 PAM
4
5
6
7

TENNIS
1 SUE
2 TONY
3 DEAN
4 HANA
5
6
7

ROBOT BUILDING
1 MARY
2 HANK
3 JULIO
4 DEAN
5 ROSA
6 DANA
7 MARY

HOMEWORK FUN
1 RASA
2 DEAN
3
4
5
6
7

1 What would Joe and Pam like to learn?

_____

2 What would you like to learn?

_____

3 What would Hana like to learn?

_____

4 What do you think of *Homework Fun*?

_____

5 What class is the most fun?

_____

6 Do you know how to play chess?

_____

How did I do? ☆ ☆ ☆ ☆ ☆

11 **Read and complete.**

> bones   brain   joints   muscle   organs   skeleton

Our body is an amazing machine. The ¹_____ are the frame. They make up the body's ²_____, and they protect the important ³_____ inside our bodies. Different ⁴_____, such as our shoulders, knees, and elbows allow the frame to be flexible. These are covered with ⁵_____, which pulls the body in different directions. All of the different parts of the body are amazing, but none of them can work without one thing – the ⁶_____.

172

12 **Read and number the paragraphs in order. Then listen and check.**

A If the tennis player is good, she finds the correct position and hits the ball with <u>precision</u>. If the tennis player isn't very good, she misses the ball.

B The tennis player's muscles all <u>contract</u> and make the bones and joints of her legs and arms move. Everything magically moves together.

C A tennis player is standing at the end of a tennis court. She can see a ball coming toward her, and she wants to hit it.

D The message travels down all the nerves and reaches the muscles. All the muscles get the message at the same time and get ready for <u>motion</u>.

E The tennis player's brain creates a message. It says something like, "Hey, guys, this ball is coming my way – I really need to get into the correct position to hit it." Her brain sends the message to all her nerves, telling them that she wants to hit the ball.

How did I do? ☆☆☆☆☆

13   **Look at 12. Correct the sentences.**

1   Your body tells your nerves that you want to move.

_____

2   Your joints send messages to your muscles.

_____

3   Your bones contract and get ready for motion.

_____

4   Your organs and joints move together.

_____

5   If you aren't a very good tennis player, you can hit the ball with precision.

_____

14   **Look at 12. Match the three underlined words with a definition.**

1   movement   _____

2   get smaller   _____

3   exactly right   _____

15   **Complete the sentences. Circle the correct words.**

1   Muscles, _____, and joints are the three main parts of your body's musculoskeletal system.

   a   bones   **b**   nerves   **c**   organs

2   _____ pull your bones in different directions so your body moves.

   a   Organs   **b**   Muscles   **c**   Nerves

3   Your bones protect the _____ within your body.

   a   contract   **b**   organs   **c**   relax

4   Muscles move your body by _____ and relaxing.

   a   building   **b**   contracting   **c**   sending a message

How did I do? ☆☆☆☆☆

16 **Read and match.**

1 A person who enters an event to be the best.

2 To be naturally good at something.

3 An event where people try to be the best and win a prize.

4 To show a feeling that you don't normally show.

5 To have the power to pull something towards you.

a have a talent

b release

c attract

d competitor

e competition

17 **Read and choose.**

1
Every year I enter a competition to see how many bees the winner can **[1]spit / attract**. I wear **[2]goggles / a plug** to stop them going up my nose. I also wear **[3]pants / goggles** to protect my eyes. I can **[4]stand / sit still** for a long time.

2
I can't play a guitar. It's too **[5]difficult / amazing** but I don't need to learn. I play air guitar! Every year I enter a competition to see who is the best. I spend hours **[6]releasing / practicing** in front of the mirror!

3
I love cherries. Every year I enter a competition to **[7]spit / release** a cherry pit to see how far it will go. It's **[8]fun / terrible**!

18 **Look at 17. Number the photos.**

a
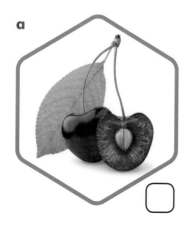

b

c

How did I do? ☆ ☆ ☆ ☆ ☆

19 Read and complete the review. Use the words from the box.

Reviewed by ¹_____

★ ★ ★ ★

A Great ²_____ for Everyone!

Kara Makes a Robot is a ³_____ movie. I watched it last ⁴_____, and I really liked it. It's not a long movie. It's only about eighty minutes, but there is a lot of great ⁵_____ in it.

It's about a girl named Kara. She ⁶_____ a robot. At first, they're friends, but soon the robot starts doing silly things. It's very funny and exciting. I don't want to tell you too much. You should watch it for ⁷_____.

Kara Makes a Robot is a great movie, and I ⁸_____ it to everyone!

acting
builds
filmgirl123
funny
Movie
night
recommend
yourself

20 Write a review of a movie, book, or TV show you like.

Reviewed by _____

_____

_____

_____

_____

_____

_____

_____

_____

How did I do? ☆ ☆ ☆ ☆ ☆

21 Read and circle ew, ay, and e_e.

> **new** gray **hay**
>
> **stew** bake eve
>
> those stay may these
>
> few

22 Underline the words with ew, ay, and e_e. Then read aloud.

1 I have a few of these gray scarves.

2 Hey, they have a new board game.

23 Connect the letters. Then write.

1 th   ew   **a** __ __ __

2 f   ese   **b** __ __ __ __ __

3 n   ay   **c** __ __ __ __

4 pr   ew   **d** __ __ __

178

24 Listen and write.

> **1** _____ three are
> **2** _____ !
> They eat **3** _____
> And wear **4** _____, too!

How did I do? ☆ ☆ ☆ ☆ ☆

25 **Look at the chart. Write questions and answers.**

What do you think of . . . ?				
Luisa	interesting	dangerous	cool	boring
Martin	difficult	amazing	boring	fun

1 What does Luisa think of drawing comic books?

<u>She thinks it's boring.</u>

2 _____

She thinks it's interesting.

3 What does Martin think of singing like a rock star?

_____

4 _____

He thinks it's amazing.

26 **Answer the questions in complete sentences.**

1 Does Karen know how to play the guitar? *(no)*

_____

2 Does Phil know how to speak Chinese? *(yes)*

_____

3 What would she like to learn? *(build a robot)*

_____

4 What would they like to learn? *(dance like a hip-hop artist)*

_____

How did I do? ☆ ☆ ☆ ☆ ☆

1 **Make guesses about Ben and ✓ the answers.**

Look at the happy and sad faces on Ben's calendar. Ben thinks some days are the best. He thinks some days are the worst.

1 What's Ben like?

☐ friendly   ☐ funny

☐ good at chess   ☐ good at sports

☐ serious   ☐ smart

2 What would Ben like to do?

☐ have a party   ☐ learn to skateboard

☐ learn to play chess   ☐ play video games

☐ watch fireworks   ☐ watch TV

Sun	Mon
Dec 31st NEW YEAR'S EVE	**Jan 1st** ?
7th LEARN HOW TO	**8th** MEET FRIENDS SHARE COLLECTION

2 **Write on Ben's calendar. Write a hobby or things for Ben to learn on the tenth and the thirteenth. Make a guess about these two days.**

3 **Look at the calendar. Make guesses and write answers.**

1 What's Ben going to do on Monday?

_____

2 What special day is on Saturday the sixth?

_____

BEN'S CALENDAR

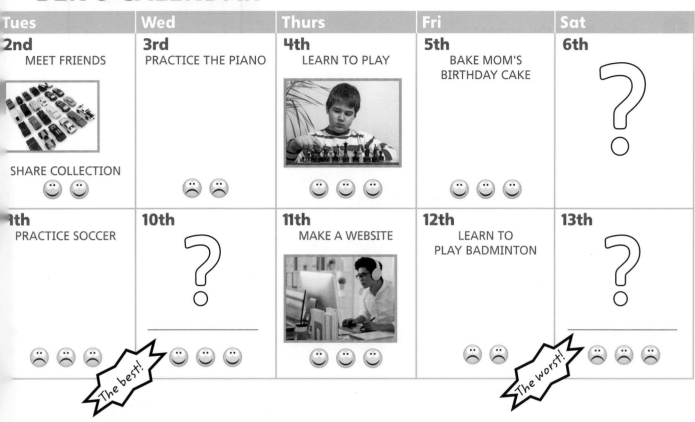

Tues	Wed	Thurs	Fri	Sat
2nd MEET FRIENDS	**3rd** PRACTICE THE PIANO	**4th** LEARN TO PLAY	**5th** BAKE MOM'S BIRTHDAY CAKE	**6th** ?
SHARE COLLECTION				
9th PRACTICE SOCCER	**10th** ? _____	**11th** MAKE A WEBSITE	**12th** LEARN TO PLAY BADMINTON	**13th** ? _____

The best!

The worst!

4 **What do you think of Ben? Would you like to be Ben's friend? Write a letter about Ben to your parents. Begin:**

Dear Mom and Dad,

I have a new classmate. His name is Ben. _____

_____

_____

_____

_____

_____

_____

Extra Grammar Practice

> Who is **taller**, Chris or Tom?   Chris is **taller than** Tom.

old	→	old**er**
big	→	big**ger**
heavy	→	heav**ier**

1   **Read. Write the answers.**

1   What is bigger? An elephant or a cat?

   An elephant is _____ a cat.

2   What is heavier? A notebook or a computer?

   A computer is _____ a notebook.

3   Who is older? Your grandmother or your aunt?

   _____

4   Who is taller? Your brother/sister or your father?

   _____

5   What is smaller? A baseball or a basketball?

   _____

> My sister's hair is longer than **my hair**.   My sister's hair is longer than **mine**.
>
> My sister's hair is longer than **your hair**.   My sister's hair is longer than **yours**.

2   **Circle the correct words.**

1   **Your / Yours** backpack is heavy. But my backpack is heavier than **your / yours**.

2   **Their / Theirs** hair is long. But my hair is longer than **their / theirs**.

3   **Her / Hers** brother is younger than **my / mine**.

4   **Our / Ours** classroom is bigger than **their / theirs** classroom.

5   **My / Mine** friend is taller than Shaun's.

6   **He / His** shoes are smaller than **her / hers** shoes.

How did I do? ☆☆☆☆☆

Extra Grammar Practice

| **Where** is | he/she | going after school? | He/She | is going to soccer practice. |
| **What** are | you | doing tonight? | We | are watching a DVD at home. |

 Look. Write What or Where. Answer the questions.

walk the dog

1 _____ is she doing after school today?

She _____.

visit the dentist

2 _____ are they going on Saturday?

They _____.

play video games

3 _____ is he doing tonight?

He _____.

go to the supermarket

4 _____ are you going in the afternoon?

We _____.

| **How often** does | he/she | have a guitar lesson? | **How often** do | you/ they | go to school? |

2 **Circle the correct questions. Write the answers.**

1 **How often do / How often does** they do the dishes?

_____ a week.

| Mon | Tues |

2 **How often do / How often does** she visit her cousins?

_____ a week.

| Sun |

How did I do?

Extra Grammar Practice

What **would** you **like**?	I**'d like** some soup.	I'd like → I would like
What **would** he/she **like**?	He**'d**/She**'d like** yogurt.	He'd/She'd like → He/She would like

1 Look. Write questions and answers.

1 What _____would she like_____ for breakfast?

_____ eggs on toast.

2 What _____ for a snack?

_____

3 _____ for dessert?

_____

Favorite Food Survey

1 Stacy: grilled cheese sandwich for breakfast

2 Martin: steamed buns for a snack

3 Stacy and Martin: yogurt with fruit for dessert

Would	you / he/she / they	**like to try** some curry?	**Yes,**	I / we / he/she / they	**would.**	**No,**	I / we / he/she / they	**wouldn't.**

2 Complete the dialog. Use the correct form of do, would, or like.

1 **A:** Does Paula like Mexican food?

B: Yes, _____.

A: _____ she _____ to try some chili?

B: Yes, she would. She loves chili.

2 **A:** Do you like hot drinks?

B: No, _____.

A: Would you like to try some lemonade?

B: No, _____. Thanks, anyway.

How did I do? ☆ ☆ ☆ ☆ ☆

Extra Grammar Practice

I		I	
You		You	
He/She	**should** eat healthy foods.	He/She	**shouldn't** stay up late.
We		We	
They		They	

1 Write sentences with should and shouldn't. Use the ideas in the boxes.

1 I have a fever.

_____

_____

> go to school today
> rest

2 Ted fell and hurt his knee.

_____

_____

> go to basketball practice
> see the school nurse

3 Some children always feel tired.

_____

_____

> watch so much TV
> get more exercise

I		**myself**.
You		**yourself**.
He/She	should take care of	**himself/herself**.
We		**ourselves**.
They		**themselves**.

2 Complete the sentences. Use herself, himself, or yourself.

1 You should take care of _____.

2 She should take care of _____.

3 He _____.

How did I do? ☆ ☆ ☆ ☆ ☆

Extra Grammar Practice

> **How many** chimpanzees were there 100 years ago?
>
> There **were** more than one million. But now there **are** only about 200,000.

1 Look at the chart and complete the sentences.

Animal	Habitat	Population in the Past	Population Now
Mexican walking fish	streams and rivers in Mexico	a lot	almost none

1 _____ Mexican walking fish ² _____ in Mexico now?

3 _____ a lot of Mexican walking fish in Mexican streams and rivers in

the past?

Now, ⁴ _____ almost none. In the past, ⁵ _____ a lot.

> **Why** are chimpanzees endangered?
>
> They're endangered **because** people are moving into their habitat.

2 Answer the questions. Use the information from the box and because.

> their habitat's polluted
> people are keeping them as pets

1 Why is the Egyptian tortoise endangered?

It's endangered _____

_____.

2 Why are Andean flamingos endangered?

_____

_____.

How did I do? ☆ ☆ ☆ ☆ ☆

Extra Grammar Practice

Did people **have** cars in 1950?	Yes, they **did**.
Did people **have** cars in 1900?	No, they **didn't**. They traveled by horse and buggy or by train.
Before TV, what **did** people **use to do** for entertainment at night?	They **used to listen** to the radio.

 1 **Read. Then answer the questions. Use did or didn't, do or don't, use or used.**

> ### Then and Now
>
> 1930s – People usually listened to the radio. They didn't own TVs.
>
> Today – People sometimes listen to the radio. Most people watch TV.
>
> 1950s – People wrote letters by hand.
>
> Today – Many people write letters on the computer.
>
> 1970s – Young people played outdoor games, like hide-and-seek.
>
> Today – Many people, young and old, play video games.

1 Did people listen to the radio years ago?

Yes, _____ because they didn't have TVs.

Do people listen to the radio now?

Yes, _____, but they usually watch TV.

2 Did people use to write letters on the computer a long time ago?

_____

Do they write letters on the computer now?

_____

3 Before video games, what _____ young people _____ to do for fun?

They _____ to play hide-and-seek outdoors.

Extra Grammar Practice

	you	going to have the party?	I	am going to have it on Monday.
When **are**			We	are going to have it on Monday.
	they		They	
When **is**	he/she	going to visit Grandma?	He/She	is going to visit her next month.
Are you/they going to visit Grandma **on the ninth**?			Yes, **on the ninth**.	
Is he/she going to visit Grandma **on the fifth**?			No, **on the ninth**.	

1 Complete the questions and answers. Use **going to** and the words from the box.

> fourth   second   third   twenty-second

1

give a present, July 2nd

When _____ your dad
_____ to your mom?
On the _____.

watch a parade, April 22nd

When _____ they
_____ a parade?
_____

3

wear different clothes, July 4th

When _____ you
_____ different clothes?
_____

4

have a party, July 3rd

When _____ you
_____ a party?
_____

2 Write in the numbers.

1 fourteenth _____   **2** eighth _____   **3** thirtieth _____   **4** first _____

How did I do? ☆☆☆☆☆

Extra Grammar Practice

Katie is a **good** chess player.	My brother's paintings are **bad**.
Katie is a **better** chess player **than** Jeff.	My sister's paintings are **worse than** his.
Katie is **the best** chess player in the class.	My paintings are **the worst** of all.

1 **Look and complete the sentences.**

1 (**big**)

	Number of shells
John	85
Mike	250
Sally	1000

John loves collecting shells. His collection is
¹_____. Mike's collection is
²_____ John's. But Sally has
³_____ in the whole class. She
started when she was six.

2 (**good**)

	Wins
Ella	10
Stephanie	4
Tania	6

Ella is good at video games. She is
¹_____ in the class. Stephanie is
a ²_____ video game player. But
Tania practices a lot. She's ³_____
Stephanie.

3 (**bad**)

	Losses
Bears	5
Tigers	3
Lions	4

The Bears, the Tigers, and the Lions are
popular baseball teams, but they are not
having a good year. The Bears team is
¹_____ of the three teams this
year. The Lions are ²_____ than
the Tigers. But the Tigers are pretty
³_____, too.

2 **Read and match.**

1 He's good   a good at climbing trees.

2 She's not very   b are bad at soccer.

3 They   c at music.

How did I do? ☆☆☆☆☆

Extra Grammar Practice

Do you **know how to play** the piano?			Yes, I do. / No, I don't.	
What **would**	you	**like to learn**?	**I'd**	**like to learn how to play** the piano.
	he/she		He**'d**/She**'d**	
	they		They**'d**	

1 **Read. Then answer the questions. Use the words from the box.**

> bake a cake   make a website   sing like a rock star

1 Jeff and Tina are going to have singing lessons next year. What would they like to learn?

_____

2 Sue loves cakes. She's having a baking class now. What would she like to learn?

_____

3 Bryan loves computers. He is having a web-design class now. What would he like to learn?

_____

What do you **think of** ballet?	I think it's boring.
What does he **think of** hip-hop music?	He thinks it's cool.

2 **Complete the dialogs.**

1 **A:** What do _____
_____?

B: I _____ it's cool.

2 **A:** What does _____
_____?

B: She _____ it's a lot of fun.

How did I do? ☆ ☆ ☆ ☆ ☆

Pearson Education Limited
KAO Two
KAO Park
Harlow
Essex
CM17 9NA
England
and Associated Companies throughout the world.

www.pearsonelt.com/bigenglish2

© Pearson Education Limited 2017

Authorised adaptation from the United States edition entitled Big English, 1st Edition, by Mario Herrera and Christopher Sol Cruz. Published by Pearson Education Inc. © 2013 by Pearson Education, Inc.

The right of Mario Herrera and Christopher Sol Cruz to be identified as the authors of this Work have been asserted by them in accordance with the Copyright, Designs and Patents Act 1988.

First published 2017
Thirteenth impression 2022

ISBN: 978-1-2922-3331-4

Set in Heinemann Roman
Printed in Slovakia by Neografia

Acknowledgements
The publisher would like to thank the following for their kind permission to reproduce their photographs:

(Key: b-bottom; c-centre; l-left; r-right; t-top)

123RF.com: 14/3, 43, 78/1, Anna-Mari West 44, Cathy Yeulet 17t, Iakov Filimonov 56tc, 61/5, 63/2, Rob Marmion 14b, Hongqi Zhang 110r, Дмитрий Гооль 98l; **Alamy Stock Photo:** Amanda Ahn 72t, Anyka 90 (artist), H Armstrong Roberts 64bl, 77r, Jon Berkeley 52/2, 61/1, Blend Images 23, 29t, 122tl, blickwinkel 58tl, Brand Z 64cr (bottom), 77l, Danita Delimont 10 (a), Design Pics Inc 52/1, 56b, 61/3, dpa picture alliance archive 58bl, Chuck Eckert 14/2, Raga Jose Fuste 84, GL Archive 64tc, Jeff Greenberg 102/6, Jim Henderson 10 (e), Juice Images 10 (c), Ernie Janes 96 (d), johnrochaphoto 90c (chess), 115tr, Ladi Kirn 122bl, Robert Landau 64tl, H Lefebvre 64c, Lordprice Collection 96 (a), Jeff Morgan 96 (b), Nature Picture Library 52/3, 56bc, 61/4, Michael Newman 2/4, David Page 14/1, 83, Ingolf Pompe 72br, RF Images 90 (dancing), RGB Ventures LLC DBA Superstock 98r, RIA Novosti 72bl, Pep Roig 70c, SAGAPhoto.com / Roux Olivier 102/2, 113r, Ian Shaw 2/3, The Africa Image Library 52/4, Vintage Images 64cl, Stacy Walsh Rosenstock 78/6, Wave Royalty Free / Design Pics Inc 64bc, World History Archive 110c; **Fotolia.com:** Alexander 14/5, allocricetulus 48cl, ameli k 90 (coin album), 114br, anankkml 61/2, Artranq 64tr, Benicce 64cr (top), bit24 48b, Blend Images 2/1, Jacek Chabraszewski 17 (b), 34, 42r, 10 (soccer), chasingmoments 5b, 17 (c), 42l, CJPhoto 90 (russian dolls), clearviewstock 90 (singing), Nina Dezhda 26 (g), DMM Photography Art 6 (c), DragonImages 102/4, 113l, 115b, Flowerpower 122tr, freestyleone 6 (f), 39tl, Joe Gough 26 (c), 26 (h), 29cl, 39tc, 39bl, haveseen 52/5, 3/1, highwaystarz 14/6, Jarp 39br, jjpixs 18, kazakovmaksim 58br, Ivan mit 90 (shells), Fabio Lotti 61/6, Monkey Business 13l, 17/1, 103b, nami66 7/3, Anna Omelchenko 13r, 17 (a), 103t, poonsap 26 (e), 39tr, rpo7 58tr, chlierner 48cr, Uryadnikov Sergey 56t, 60, WavebreakmediaMicro 76, dward Westmacott 48t, Alexander Yakovlev 102/8; **Getty Images:** eter Dazeley 10 (d), ewg3D 10 (b), Jupiterimages 78/2, KidStock 3r, mos Morgan 3l; **Pearson Education Ltd:** Studio 8 5c, Jon Barlow 107bl; **PhotoDisc:** Alan D Carey 63/3; **Shutterstock.com:** Peter Albrektsen 90 ars), 115tl, Alexandr Junek Imaging 107br, AVAVA 90 (video game), bds cl (bottom), bikeworldtravel 78/3, Franck Boston 35, Steve Bower 8, heryl Casey 91, Sam Chadwick 70t, Everett Collection 64br, Mike Flippo t, fusebulb 47 (a), Mandy Godbehear 78/5, Warren Goldswain 11, 113cr, ris Harvey 98c, Charlie Hutton 70b, Dmitry Kalinovsky 14/4, Kamira 90 riting), Sebastian Kaulitzki 47 (c), Anna Kucherova 110l, Lukasz Kurbiel , Lara65 90 (basketball), Lebendkulturen.de 47 (d), Littlekidmoment 2/5, Olga Miltsova 26 (a), 29cr, Monkey Business Images 78/4, 122br, kkytok 47 (b), papkin 26 (d), 29b, Denis Radovanovic 102/3, 113cl, 114bl, l, Julian Rovagnati 64cl (top), Shchipkova Elena 2/2, Slawek Radek

107t, stockyimages 45, tacar 26 (b), Leah-Anne Thompson 15, TunedIn by Westend61 5t, Peter Weber 102/7, 124r, wormdog 49, www.BillionPhotos.com 102/1, yalayama 19, ZouZou 17/2

Cover images: Front: *Getty Images:* JGI / Jamie Grill

All other images © Pearson Education

Every effort has been made to trace the copyright holders and we apologise in advance for any unintentional omissions. We would be pleased to insert the appropriate acknowledgement in any subsequent edition of this publication.

Illustrated by
Sean@KJA-Artists, Matt Latchford, Victor Moshopoulos, Zaharias Papadopoulos (Hyphen) Jamie Pouge, Q2A Media Services and Christos Skaltsas (Hyphen).

Tracklist

Class CD track number	Workbook CD track number	Unit and activity number
11	2	Unit 1, activity 3
15	3	Unit 1, activity 7
17	4	Unit 1, activity 14
23	5	Unit 1, activity 27
30	6	Unit 2, activity 3
34	7	Unit 2, activity 7
36	8	Unit 2, activity 15
42	9	Unit 2, activity 28
49	10	Unit 3, activity 3
53	11	Unit 3, activity 7
54	12	Unit 3, activity 9
56	13	Unit 3, activity 14
63	14	Unit 3, activity 25
70	15	Unit 4, activity 3
74	16	Unit 4, activity 7
76	17	Unit 4, activity 13
82	18	Unit 4, activity 25
88	19	Unit 5, activity 2
92	20	Unit 5, activity 6
94	21	Unit 5, activity 11
100	22	Unit 5, activity 23
106	23	Unit 6, activity 3
110	24	Unit 6, activity 7

Class CD track number	Workbook CD track number	Unit and activity number
112	25	Unit 6, activity 14
118	26	Unit 6, activity 25
126	27	Unit 7, activity 3
130	28	Unit 7, activity 7
133	29	Unit 7, activity 12
139	30	Unit 7, activity 24
146	31	Unit 8, activity 2
150	32	Unit 8, activity 5
151	33	Unit 8, activity 8
153	34	Unit 8, activity 10
159	35	Unit 8, activity 20
166	36	Unit 9, activity 3
170	37	Unit 9, activity 7
172	38	Unit 9, activity 12
178	39	Unit 9, activity 24